The Voices of Children in the Bible

Rita B. Hays

WestBow
PRESS
A DIVISION OF THOMAS NELSON

ISBN: 978-1-4497-4748-0 (e)
ISBN: 978-1-4497-4747-3 (sc)
ISBN: 978-1-4497-4749-7 (hc)

Library of Congress Control Number: 2012906436

WestBow Press books may be ordered through booksellers or by contacting:

WestBow Press
A Division of Thomas Nelson
1663 Liberty Drive
Bloomington, IN 47403
www.westbowpress.com
1-(866) 928-1240

Printed in the United States of America

WestBow Press rev. date: 4/30/2012

To the children of
Connell Memorial United Methodist Church
Goodlettsville, Tennessee

"Finally, my friends keep your minds on whatever is true, pure, right, holy, friendly, and proper. Don't ever stop thinking about what is truly worthwhile and worthy of praise."
Philippians 4:8 (Contemporary English Version)

Contents

Contents

Introduction

Varied voices speak to us in scripture. The faithful voices of men and women ring out in both the Old Testament and the New Testament as believers share their failures, their triumphs, and above all, their faithfulness in a God of forgiveness, love, and mercy. Moses' voice demanded freedom for his people. Prophetic voices summon us to new ways of thinking and doing. The wisdom writers' voices offer sound, practical advice for everyday living. The voice of John the Baptist cries out, chastising us for our sins and prodding us toward repentance. The gospel writers heralded the voice of Jesus as teacher, healer, Messiah, and Savior. The evangelistic voice of the apostle Paul and the voices of early church leaders provide direction and guidance for communities of faith in all generations.

Men and women of faith speak with myriad voices. We listen. When we listen, we hear our own voices. We relate to the suffering voices, the comforting voices, the glad voices, the courageous voices, and the visionary voices. These passionate adult voices compel us to worship, to praise, to rejoice, and to believe. Where, however, are the voices of children in the variety of voices we encounter in scripture?

The poignant voices of children are present in scripture, strong voices that demand to be heard! So, why have we not heard them? Often, they are overshadowed and diminished by the adult voices that speak alongside them in a particular text. Sometimes they are not heard because we, as adults, are not listening. Other times, they are ignored, viewed by some as irrelevant and unimportant. Now is the time to recognize, affirm, and value the voices of children in the Bible, voices that prove to be instrumental to the outcome of a particular story. Biblical readers must not stifle the pivotal voices of children, but instead hear them with renewed minds, fresh eyes, and open hearts.

This book seeks to lift up the voices of children in both the Old and

New Testaments. Twelve stories highlight the voices of these children, showing the ways in which select children play a significant role in the outcome of the narrative. Additionally, readers receive insight into ways they can relate to children today and also relevant lessons they can learn, based upon the biblical text. Readers are urged to listen carefully to these children, for in their forceful speech and courageous actions, readers might discover their own brave voices. In hearing and understanding the truth in these children's voices, readers are inspired to follow their example and engage in their own acts of devoted witness to God. These children teach us that we serve a parent God who blesses all of God's children with the gift of voice. Like these children, we only need to speak up and use our voices for good.

Rita B. Hays
Nashville, Tennessee

PART ONE:
Stories From The Old Testament

A Child Speaks Out

Read the Story: 2 Kings 5:2–19

> *She said to her mistress, "If only my lord*
> *were with the prophet who is in Samaria!*
> *He would cure him of his leprosy."*
>
> 2 Kings 5:3 (NRSV)

Mary Jane, a fifth grader, attends the elementary school located near her home in a suburban neighborhood. As an avid learner, an excellent student, and a popular child, she enjoys school. Mary Jane's outgoing personality and compassionate nature garner her many friends and the equal affection and trust of her teachers and peers. Recently, however, one incident at school proves to be a challenge for this vivacious child. Mary Jane observes the bullying of one of her classmates by a boy in her school. The bullying boy frequently steals the lunch money of the victimized child, teases the young boy with disparaging remarks, and threatens any child who dares to tell on him.

Mary Jane finds herself caught in a dilemma. Should she tell her teacher or remain silent? Mary Jane knows what her parents would tell her to do. They have taught her from an early age to show compassion and love toward others, especially those who suffer. Mary Jane also knows how her church leaders and friends would advise her to handle the situation. Her church has taught her from early childhood to practice the Golden Rule, to act toward others in the same way she wishes to be treated. Just recently, her church leaders taught a series of lessons to the children on the harmful effects of bullying and the duty of Christian believers to take a stand for righteousness and justice.

After a discussion with her parents and her pastor, Mary Jane decides to tell her schoolteacher what is happening with the bullying of her classmate. Since Mary Jane's teacher knows her student to be a person of integrity and trust, the teacher believes Mary Jane and shares her concerns with the principal. Mary Jane's courageous actions and truthful words result in action by school officials. They work to correct the bullying situation for the betterment of the boy who is being bullied. Mary Jane desires no recognition; she simply speaks the truth out of love, care, and concern for the victim.

Second Kings, chapter 5, relates the powerful story of the healing of Naaman, a greatly respected and high-ranking military official in the Syrian army of King Aram. Afflicted with the dreaded disease of leprosy, Naaman found healing only after he obeyed the instructions of the prophet Elisha. Sermons, commentaries, and lessons on this biblical story most often center on the healing of Naaman by the great prophet, the lesson of humility learned by the skilled commander, and Naaman's amazing discovery that the God of Israel is greater than any other god. A few fleeting comments are made about the words of the unnamed servant girl. Only mentioned hastily, her actions and words are passed over quickly so the writer or speaker can get to the real heart of the story. We fail to realize how important and life-changing her words and actions proved to be in the outcome of our story. After all, it is easy to overlook and silence the voice of a child, particularly a lowly servant girl. Yet, her voice yearns and demands to be heard. Also, her bravery must be allowed to emerge from the pages of the biblical text. Just as the actions of Naaman leap out at the readers, until we are fully immersed in his intriguing story, the action of the servant girl also provide the reader with an interesting narrative. The voice of this servant girl should be heard alongside the voices of the prophet and also the voice of the commander. Her words and actions proved to be pivotal in the outcome of our narrative. A bold child spoke with clarity and truth. Is it not time to grant this servant girl the credit she deserves?

So we take time to hear her voice in our current day. We allow her to speak, and we listen carefully. We do not interrupt her, as adults often are prone to do when engaging children in conversation. And when she finishes speaking, we discover that there are lessons from her story for us to learn and to apply in our conversations with children today. For we garner from her words and actions important truths about the voices and motives of children in our present time, and also our need to listen carefully to their voices whenever they speak with the same passion, honesty, and conviction.

Let us begin with her story, a story of captivity and slavery. The Hebrew word to describe the young Israelite girl is *qutan*, which means "diminutive in age or importance." This girl was both. The Bible informs us that she was a young servant girl. The Hebrew word used is *naarah*, depicting a girl between the ages of infancy and adolescence. We do not know her exact age or her name, but we know she was a child. She was diminutive not only in age, but in importance as well. This Jewish child had been taken prisoner by the Syrian nation during one of its raids on the nation of Israel. She served the wife of Naaman, the commander of the king's army. As a slave, she lived under the authority of Naaman and his wife. When the young girl learned of her master's disease, she knew she could very easily say nothing and go about her household chores. Yet she acted with compassion toward the very people who enslaved her in a foreign land. Her Jewish upbringing taught her to care about others even in the midst of her own persecution and slavery.

Early in its history, the Jewish nation sensed a call from God to treat others with hospitality. Hospitality was required not just for family and friends, but for strangers and foreigners as well. This young girl had been taught to treat others with compassion from the time she was born, a lesson she carried with her into her present situation. She also possessed a faith in God and a trust and respect for the prophets of her nation, Israel.

The girl shared with Naaman's wife her confidence in the healing powers of the prophet Elisha. She convinced her mistress that her husband should seek out Elisha, as he had healing powers. She believed that he could cure her master's leprosy. Her actions and words took courage on her part. Would a servant's word be considered valid? Would her mistress listen to her? Even if her mistress did listen, could she convince her husband to follow the advice of a slave girl? After all, this girl was only a child. Yet apparently the young girl already had proven that she could be trusted. If this child had failed to speak, Naaman would never have known about the ability of the prophet Elisha to cure his leprosy. Thus, the rest of our story would be void.

Apparently, this servant girl possessed the art of persuasion due to her trustworthy and dependable character. Naaman not only believed what his wife conveyed to him about Elisha, but he was also willing to go to the king of Syria and ask for his permission to speak with the king of Israel. Naaman carried letters from the king of Syria asking the Jewish king to offer help. The Syrian king humbled himself in making this request of a Jewish king. The Syrians opposed Israel with a vengeance. They failed to show any respect for the Israelite nation, its kings, and its God. If Naaman doubted the words of the servant girl or failed to trust his wife's belief in the girl's words, he would never have put his king in a position of having to ask the Israelite king for his help. Naaman took a great risk when he trusted the words of the servant girl.

Some might argue that Naaman reached the point in his illness where he found himself desperate. Thus, he clung to any measure of hope. His situation was so urgent that he was willing to try anything, even trusting in the words of a child! This argument, however, should not lessen or negate in any way the bravery of the servant girl and her pivotal role in our story. Her words set in motion the rest of the action in the biblical narrative. Her words were decisive. Without her speaking out, Naaman might have suffered for many years, never knowing of the prophet Elisha and his ability to offer him healing in the name of God. Furthermore, Naaman would never have come to know of the power of God and never have recognized the God of Israel as the one true God. While the words of the servant girl offered her master the opportunity for healing, it was her faith that brought true healing. Only her faith in God and in the healing power of the prophet Elisha motivated this child to speak out. She believed her master could and would be healed if he took the right steps.

The biblical text provides no insight, but one has to believe that God continued to work in Naaman's life even when he returned to his own nation. Naaman admitted to Elisha that his duties as commander of the Syrian army compelled him to worship the Syrian god Rimmon. The Syrian king expected Naaman to accompany him to the house of Rimmon for worship. Naaman begged forgiveness from God, and Elisha sent him forth in peace. Elisha understood Naaman's situation, but realized that God works in mysterious ways. Both Elisha and the servant girl believed in a God of revelation, a God whose being and nature manifested itself over time. The story ends with the hope that Naaman gradually grew in his understanding of God.

The exchange between Elisha and Naaman took place because a child showed no fear and spoke out. Naaman came to recognize the power of God through the prophet Elisha, but only because of the initiative of a servant girl. She deserves credit for her courage, her compassion, and her willingness to speak words that led to action and change.

All of us know children in our own lives who possess many of the commendable characteristics of this young slave girl. These children sometimes find themselves in situations where they are compelled to speak out for change. It is easy for us, as adults, to fail to listen to the words of children, trust their voices and actions, follow through on their advice, and recognize the faith that guides them. What a difference it makes in our world and in the life of trustworthy, dependable children when parents, teachers, pastors, and friends take the time to listen to them and take them seriously!

Our story at the beginning of this chapter provides for us a good example of the way one child spoke out against injustice and made a difference in the life of a bullied child. This child spoke out boldly. Her teacher listened to her because she has proven herself trustworthy in her past actions. More than likely, the teacher took the time to verify what Mary Jane shared concerning the bullying situation at her school. Her teacher checked to make sure Mary Jane provided accurate information. Yet the teacher showed Mary Jane a great deal of respect when taking the time to stop and listen to her words. When the teacher discovered that Mary Jane told the truth, the teacher followed up, along with the principal. These authorities then took proper and swift action to correct the bullying situation. Their quick action conveyed to Mary Jane that her teacher and principal took her seriously, honored her word, and found her to be a person of integrity. This helped shape Mary Jane's own self-worth and strengthened her trust in adults. She learned that she could confide in others without fear of reprimand or disbelief.

Like Mary Jane's teacher and the young servant girl's mistress, adults need to listen carefully to the words of children. We communicate to children that we really love and respect them when we truly stop and listen carefully to their words. We show children a disservice when we interrupt their conversations or add our own interpretations, which may or may not be correct. Children easily pick up on the body language of adults. When they observe adults fidgeting, looking off in the distance, or finishing their sentences for them, children quickly understand that these people are not really interested in what they have to say. Talking with and listening to children takes patience. Children often take their time to convey what is in their hearts and on their minds. Adults must give children their full attention and listen carefully to what they say.

Granted, some children, like some adults, are more trustworthy and dependable than others. Most individuals are fully aware of those people in whom they can trust and depend and whose word proves to be honest. We know those in our lives who are people of integrity. Children understand our need to check out their stories, especially if their demands involve a radical change. Sometimes a request requires verification. We do not dishonor a child when we search compassionately for the validity of his or her words. Adults should be sensitive not to hurt children when doing so. Children need assurance that adults believe what they are saying is the truth, if this is the case. We can explain to them that sometimes conversations have to be explored in greater depth and investigated for further details. When we discover that children are telling the truth and a change needs to take place, we need to communicate with them. We should offer them assurance that we believe them and appreciate their courage in communicating with us. If we discover children's words are untruthful, we are obligated to address that matter with them as well.

Often children feel betrayed when adults listen to them, but take little or no action to remedy a situation. If Naaman's wife had only listened to her servant girl, but failed to communicate her words to her husband, the outcome of the story would have been very different. She acted on the words of the young girl. The mistress followed through by sharing her slave's words with her husband. No doubt, she also made sure that Naaman took action by contacting the Syrian king. Our story would have a different ending if Naaman had failed to take his wife's advice. Children want to be taken seriously and they appreciate it when adults not only listen to what they are sharing, but follow through when actions are necessary. Children gain a sense of pride and self-respect when their words carry influence with others. They grow in self-worth when their sharing with dependable adults leads to action that brings about worthwhile change.

Although separated by time and divided by differing circumstances, both the servant girl and Mary Jane acted on their faith in God. Their faith taught them to live as people of honesty, compassion, and hospitality. Their faith inspired them to reach out to the suffering. Their faith compelled them to speak words of healing. Their faith called them to alleviate hurt. Their faith motivated them to act as channels of God's grace. Children can rarely do these things alone; they need the help of caring adults who listen and take action alongside them in the journey of faith.

Both the stories of the servant girl and Mary Jane found their true meaning in community. The servant girl's honest and passionate words of hope and healing came to fruition only when believed by those who possessed the authority to put her words into action: Naaman, his wife, Elisha, and the kings. Mary Jane's forceful and pleading words spilled forth as cries of help for a hurting classmate. They came to a crescendo only when those who claimed that they had a responsibility and duty to protect children from harm took her words seriously. Both children spoke out with boldness. Both children spoke words of power. Adults listened to their words!

Children today have words to speak. These children speak with courage, with fervor, and with hope. They so desperately want to be heard. They yearn for a community of caring adults with open ears. Are we listening?

QUESTIONS FOR REFLECTION AND DISCUSSION

1. How might the outcome of our Bible story been different had the young servant girl not spoken out?

2. Think of the children you know in your church, home, and community who have the same brave characteristics of the servant girl in our biblical story. Talk about these children, and lift up their names in thanksgiving to God.

3. Name some situations today that may require children to take a stand for what is right.

4. Discuss some risky situations children encounter each day.

5. What can parents do to teach children about issues of justice and righteousness?

6. What can churches do to teach children about issues of justice and righteousness?

7. How can churches help children in risky or dangerous situations?

8. Name and discuss some situations you are aware of in which children you know have acted with bravery and courage. Name these children, and offer a prayer of thanksgiving.

9. In what ways do adults today fail to truly listen to the voices of children? In what ways do adults stifle the voices of children?

10. Share some listening skills that might help you when engaging in a conversation with a child.

A Child Takes Action

Read the Story: Exodus 2:1–10

> *Then his sister said to Pharaoh's daughter,*
> *"Shall I go and get you a nurse from the*
> *Hebrew women to nurse the child for you?"*
> *Pharaoh's daughter said to her, "Yes." So*
> *the girl went and called the child's mother.*
>
> Exodus 2:7–8 (NRSV)

MeriAllen Krueger, an active member of the children's ministry at Connell Memorial United Methodist Church, brings a unique approach to every one of her birthday parties. Each year when her birthday rolls around, MeriAllen refuses to receive gifts for her own benefit. Rather, she plans her party around the needs of others. She instructs the children who attend her party to bring money for a designated mission rather than spend it on gifts for her.

One year, the birthday money she received went to Room in the Inn, an agency that helps homeless people in her community. Another year, MeriAllen contributed the money to a fund to help purchase a sound system for the church nursery, so the caregivers could hear the worship service. This child also donated money to help with flood relief. Some of her gift money went to support her sister, who has arthritis. In addition, her money was used to sponsor her sister's annual walk team, Ana-Carlin's Crew 4 A Cure.

MeriAllen takes action rather than sitting on the sidelines and watching. She believes that God calls her to be present in alleviating suffering and easing the burdens of others. She places the needs of God's children above her own desire for material gifts. She does not believe that reaching out to the needy is only the responsibility of adults; rather, she proves that children have a pivotal role to play in mission and outreach.

MeriAllen could easily have taken the attitude that adults should step up and take care of all of these things she involves herself in as a giver. She might reason that adults could take care of the sound system in the nursery, adults should give money to help the homeless, adults would offer aid to flood victims, and adults might support her sister's worthy cause. However, MeriAllen refuses to distance herself from the needs of the world. She discovers that, along with adults, she can make a positive difference in the lives of others. So she does not hesitate to get involved. She gives freely, with a heart of gratitude and humility.

MeriAllen learns her lessons of stewardship from many sources. Her parents, Glenn and Caroline, taught her, from an early age, the valuable lessons of sharing, compassion, and love. Her Sunday school teachers and pastors reinforce parental teachings through stories and examples of Christlike giving and service. Nurtured both in her home and church to be a steward of her God-given gifts and abilities, MeriAllen puts into practice what she learns and does so with grace. She steps out of her comfort zone to help others. She is an action-taker!

Like MeriAllen, we discover that the child Miriam in our Old Testament story proved to be an action-taker. We learn her intriguing story in the book of Exodus. Miriam lived at a time in which the Jewish people found themselves slaves to the powerful Egyptian nation. The current king of Egypt feared the strength of the Jewish people. He worried about the increasingly growing number of Jewish slaves in his kingdom, so he ordered that all Jewish boy babies be killed. When Miriam's mother gave birth to her son, she placed him in a papyrus basket and gently set him in the Nile River. Miriam carefully watched her brother from a distance. When Pharaoh's daughter discovered the baby boy and wanted him as her own, Miriam rushed from her hiding place to offer to secure a nursemaid for the child. Wise Miriam recruited her own mother, who nursed the child Moses until he was weaned and ready to live at the royal court.

We understand Miriam's bravery when we realize that she was only a child. The New Revised Standard version of the Bible uses the word *girl* to describe her. The Hebrew writers and editors used various classification to describe the feminine, including *child, girl, virgin, betrothed,* and *young woman.* The use of the word *girl* in the biblical account holds significance for the reader in understanding Miriam's age range. The term *girl* refers to a child who is much younger in age than a *young woman,* who has reached the age acceptable for marriage. When the scripture refers to Miriam as a *girl,* that lets us know that she had not experienced the onset of puberty. Most scholars place Miriam's age somewhere between seven years to eleven years.

The child demonstrated her courage when she stepped forward out of her hiding place and approached Pharaoh's daughter. Miriam belonged to a group of people enslaved by the princess' father. Miriam took action and spoke out boldly even though she was uncertain whether she would be listened to or taken seriously. The princess could very easily have rejected Miriam's request, chided Miriam for only being a child, insulted her as a Jewish slave, or even worse, entirely dismissed her words as the mere babbling of a young girl. She could have criticized Miriam and asked her to immediately leave her royal presence. Yet something about Miriam's demeanor caught the attention of Pharaoh's daughter. Miriam apparently presented herself as a reliable, trustworthy child. Miriam risked her own safety for the security of her infant brother.

Miriam sprang into action with her sharp thinking. She possessed wisdom far greater than her age. Many adults and children in a similar circumstance might easily become frightened and not think clearly. Not Miriam, however. Miriam quickly assessed the situation and offered a practical, wise, and clever suggestion. She determined a need and worked to find a solution that saved her brother from death and, at the same time, appeased the princess. Miriam's quick thinking allowed Miriam's family to continue to have a pivotal role in the life of their infant son. Miriam also, with certainty, secured the safety of her baby brother. If Pharaoh's daughter decreed that Miriam's family would take care of Moses until he was weaned, then no harm would come to Moses or to Miriam or her family. Her wit, bravery, and clear thinking outsmarted Pharaoh's cruel edict.

Readers enjoy this biblical story because it centers on Moses, the great Jewish leader, and gives us details about his infancy. The story intrigues us, and we are drawn to its poignant details. We focus on Moses in a basket, floating on the Nile River, and then his discovery and rescue by Pharaoh's daughter. How often we forget the pivotal role that Miriam played in our story. Moses' actions capture the attention of biblical readers. Moses' popularity often overshadows Miriam's actions. After all, Moses became the great deliverer of the Jewish people. God called him to save the Jewish people and convince the pharaoh to release them from captivity. Yet without Miriam's actions, Moses would never have become the leader he was destined to be. Miriam allowed Moses to begin his early years in the household of his heritage and birth.

No doubt his family formed his thinking even in infancy. Even though he would later be influenced by Egyptian ideas, his own family also molded him. They sang to him lullabies about Yahweh. They taught him Jewish customs and laws. They instilled in him a yearning for justice. They told him stories about his own people and their struggles for freedom. Children learn many lessons in infancy that remain with them throughout their lifetime. Surely Moses' family shaped his mind and heart at an early age.

Let us give Miriam the credit due her. We must not skip hurriedly over her story so that we can get to the story of Moses. Both Moses and Miriam were heroes. Both deserve their place in the freedom song of the Jewish people. Miriam often takes second place to Moses. We need to stop and read her story. We ought to ponder her valuable part in the biblical narrative of deliverance. We must come to appreciate her bold actions, for they are pivotal in the outcome of the story. We should take the time to listen to her wise voice and comprehend her courageous actions. She was only a child, but the steps she took to save her brother proved that she was mature beyond her age.

The way we treat and view Miriam has consequences for the way we treat and view children today who want to step out in faith and engage in risk-taking mission and service—the children we know, like Miriam, have gifts to share. Our story of MeriAllen Krueger is only one of many examples of the way children, impacted by their faith, start reaching out to others. When children are nurtured to show compassion, when they are taught to extend hospitality, and when they are inspired to share their love of God and neighbors, then, like Miriam, they too take action.

Children today reach out in a variety of ways to show the grace of God to others. Stop and look around at the children you know. Watch for ways they are practicing good stewardship and thoughtful service to others. Take time to affirm their actions. Tell these children you appreciate them. Covenant to pray for them. Offer to partner with them. Also, tell their stories. Let others in the faith community know about the actions of children that make a difference in the church, the community, and the world. Doing so instills in children a sense of worth and inspires them to continue to do good deeds.

Like with Miriam, many of the humble and unselfish actions of children today go unnoticed. Too often, children are told that they are too young to accomplish much, but this is far from the truth. Children need positive and affirming words from caring adults. They also yearn for adults to set an example for them and allow them to work alongside faith mentors. What a difference it can make to a child if adults will take the time to teach him or her how to give generously and then grant him or her the opportunity to put what she learned into practice.

Miriam provides us a biblical example of a child who took action at a decisive time in the history of her people. Rather than rush quickly over her story, it is time for us to embrace her narrative. The story brings to light the actions of one child who appeared in no way to be afraid to seize her opportunity and moment in history. Without fear, out of her hiding place she stepped and made a decision that proved to be decisive for the history of her people. Miriam refused to give in to the oppressive powers around her. She possessed strength, fortitude, and determination. She challenged the system of injustice. She turned evil into good. Her story becomes the story of many children we know today, repeated time and again when faith motivates a child to take an action that makes a difference in the world.

Miriam's voice stirs us to take a stand in our time and place. Miriam's wisdom inspires us to work for righteous change. Miriam's passionate plea becomes our own. We must never bury Miriam's story or think it less valuable than that of brother Moses. Rather, we must let it rise from the pages of the biblical narrative to impact us. For her story reads like numerous stories of children we know today. They are the children who follow Miriam's example. They too are action-takers in their world. Their stories intertwine with Miriam's. Their narratives, like Miriam's, refuse to be neglected and ignored. For like Miriam, who left her secure hiding place to venture boldly into the Egyptian sunlight, our children yearn to join her in their own risky adventures of faith. Surely our response to their questioning and seeking voices might be the same as that of Pharaoh's daughter. We honestly and simply reply yes!

QUESTIONS FOR REFLECTION AND DISCUSSION

1. Discuss how you think Miriam felt as she made her decision to approach Pharaoh's daughter. What characteristics did Miriam possess that allowed her to take action?

2. Share the story of any child who has taken risky action in order to help a sibling or family member.

3. Discuss the children you know who have the same courage, bravery, and determination as Miriam exhibited. Name them, and offer a time of thanksgiving to God for these children.

4. Discuss ways you have seen children in your community or in the school setting reaching out to others in need.

5. Discuss ways you have seen children in your congregation engaging in risk-taking mission and service. Name some projects and mission activities the children have participated in that have been effective.

6. Discuss ways the home and church can teach children to show compassion and caring for others.

7. How can adults partner with children in sharing with others? Can you name some examples of the way adults in your congregation work alongside children in mission and outreach activities?

8. Think about some of the children you know who act with compassion toward others and go out of their way to practice caring acts of love. Names these children, and offer a prayer of thanksgiving for their examples of unselfish giving.

9. What are some mission and outreach activities in your congregation in which you allow children to participate?

10. What are some projects and activities families can do together that will teach children how to reach out to others?

A Child Risks His Life

Read the Story: I Samuel 17:19–50

> *You come to me with sword and spear and*
> *javelin; but I come to you in the name of*
> *the Lord of hosts, the God of the armies of*
> *Israel, whom you have defied.*

I Samuel 17:45

Each year, St Joseph Hospital, located in Tampa, Florida, proudly announces their Kids Are Heroes winners. The distinguished list includes children as young as five years of age. The honorees are recognized for their heroic deeds or distinguished acts of selfless courage. Many of the recipients risked their lives to save others.[1]

Take, for example, hero and heroine Colton Shephard and Julianne Ramirez. Both children undoubtedly deserved the prestigious recognition they received. While walking home from school, Colton witnessed a car accident. The car caught on fire, trapping a woman and child inside. Colton bravely kicked out the windshield, cleared away the broken glass, and risked his own life by pulling the child and woman out of the car. He then faithfully stayed with the injured until paramedics arrived. Julianne rescued a young child who nearly drowned in a swimming pool. She acted quickly, jumped in the water, and pulled the sinking child out of the pool. The heroine started CPR, which she learned through Girl Scouts. Julianne received credit for saving the child's life. Other risk-taking honorees included a child who saved his sibling from a dog attack and another who called 911 to help her relative suffering from a heart attack.[2]

The book of Samuel contains a remarkable story of another heroic child who risked his life to save others. The story of David and Goliath proves to be one of the favorite stories of Bible readers. They are captured by the vivid action in the narrative and the courageous antics of a child hero, David. They find it easy to cheer for the underdog as he was facing none other than a nine-foot giant! The scripture never tells us David's exact age, but we know that his youth prevented him from serving in the Israelite army. Therefore, we can determine that David was indeed a child when this story took place.

The reader's understanding of the story is enhanced when we gain knowledge of the background. Gaining clarity about the facts of the story also helps us more fully appreciate David's heroic actions. We cannot leave our story without concluding that David was indeed a hero, as brave and valiant as any adult we encounter in scripture.

Let's begin with some background information. The nation of Israel faced a crisis of paramount proportion. The army of the Philistine, Israel's dreaded enemy, sought to cripple the nation of Israel. Israel's army and the enemy faced each other, camped out on opposite sides of a valley. Both sides remained alert and ready for battle. Day after day, the nine-foot Philistine giant Goliath taunted the Israelite nation. No one dared stop his jeering out of fear. No one except a child, that is. David stepped into the picture when he arrived on the battlefield to bring supplies to his older brothers who served in the army. He bravely volunteered to fight Goliath. However, convincing King Saul to allow him to fight took all of David's powers of persuasion. David reminded Saul that he worked as a sheep keeper and often protected his sheep when wild animals attacked. His past heroic actions as a shepherd boy reflected his courage and bravery in that moment of critical need.

Isn't it interesting that once David gained Saul's approval, Saul immediately imposed his adult thinking upon the situation? He outfitted David with his own armor, sword, and helmet. David looked ridiculous and struggled to even walk. David resorted to the familiar: his own staff, five smooth stones, his slingshot, and his shepherd's pouch. These possessions served him well in the past and they would serve him well at that moment in history. David refused to pretend to be someone he was not. He returned to his shepherd identity and rejected the image of warrior. David believed God helped him in his endeavor.

The Israelite people believed God sanctioned and blessed their numerous military operations, for they conceived of themselves as a nation selected by God for victory in battle. When Goliath mocked the Israelite army, he ridiculed Yahweh, the true commander-in-chief of the Israelite's warfare. This concept of war helps us better understand David's passionate desire to serve his nation and defend its honor. David's daring mission defended the integrity of his people against those who wished to ridicule the God of Israel. He took a stand for what he believed and prevented the total humiliation of his nation when a formidable opponent threatened.

Fortunately, throughout history, David's voice has not been neglected. This is one biblical story focused on a child where his voice and actions have been heard loudly and clearly. Perhaps this happened because the readers of the story were captured by the very notion of a child emerging victorious against a giant when even adult soldiers refused to battle him. Yet the beauty of the story rests in the trust David exhibited toward Yahweh. Many adults fail to turn to God in their time of need in the way David did. David truly believed that God offers help to those who struggle to fight injustice. David fought not for honor or recognition, but for what was right. He used the gifts that God endowed him with, the skills he possessed as a shepherd boy. David refused to pretend he was a seasoned soldier; rather he acted like a shepherd engaged in battle against a foe as formidable as a bear, lion, or wolf. He could not fight the giant with a warrior's tools, but he could fight the giant with his shepherd's tools. Also, he recognized that he battled not in his own strength, but in the might and power of his God, whom he totally trusted and sought to honor. He fought to maintain the respect of his nation and to uplift the name of their God.

All of us encounter giants in our lives that seek to defeat us. A child offers us important lessons on courage, fortitude, and strength for when we encounter giants in our world today. These giants take many different forms for each of us. Among them are the giants of addiction, job loss, illness, marital problems, family issues, and other crises that test our faith. We discover that these giants appear as large, vicious, and menacing as Goliath must have appeared to the Israelites. None of us can escape the giants in our lives, but David teaches us to face them, trusting in God, who is always present with us. David encourages us to seek out and turn to our faithful God, who equips us with just the right resources to face the giants, and to do so with the same determination he exhibited.

David also reminds us to use the resources that God gifts us with and accept the reality that these are the only useful tools we have to combat evil in our world today. We cannot pretend to be somebody we are not, and we cannot fight our battles with someone else's tools. We must use our own. Furthermore, David wants us to understand that our battles in life are not ours alone. They also belong to God, who fights beside us and gives us the strength to endure.

David provides us with some important truths when we consider the risks that many children encounter and face in our world. First, we must commend heroic children who have risked their lives to save others. The stories that emerge from the Kids are Heroes amaze us, but there are many other children across our world who prove to be heroes and have risked their lives to save others. If you know of such a child, you would do well to find ways to honor this child. Let your local media know about the actions of the child and lift up his or her remarkable story. This boosts a child's self-esteem and lets him know of your sincere appreciation, love, and affirmation.

There are many children who live in situations in which they must risk their lives each day just to stay alive or help family members cope. We must give these children credit as well and pray for them daily. Some children live in abusive situations where they come into harm's way each day or have family members who are abused. Sometimes these children fight back against the abuse or seek to protect siblings who get in the way of the perpetrator. If you know of such a child, it is your duty to speak out to the authorities, those who can offer protection. Often we are unaware of these situations, but we need to be alert to the possibility. There are many children who live each day with the harmful effects of child abuse, and they live in constant fear and danger.

There are other children who live in homes where they are simply neglected or not well cared-for by parents. These may be homes where parents are sick, addicted, deficient in parenting skills, or lack the money to provide good food, clothes, or medical care. These children are at risk and often spent their time wondering where their next meal will come from, if they will have clothes for school, or if their getting sick will place a hardship on the family budget. These children also risk their lives each day to stay alive. Sometimes they see no other way out of their crisis situation than to steal from others to get what they need. Many schools now serve free breakfast and lunch to these children during the school year, but when school is out, many of these children do not have proper meals. Churches and communities can partner with parents to help provide clothes, food, and medical care. They can also offer classes to improve parenting skills. Also, some communities have developed programs to feed hungry children when school is out.

People struggling with addictions are on the rise in our society today. Children are certainly not immune from the devastating effects of addiction on family life. These children live in homes where an addicted parent is often unable to properly care for them. The spouse of the addict often focuses his or her attention on the problems of the addict, and thus children suffer greatly and are often neglected. Addiction can cause parents to angrily and viciously lash out at one another and take their problems out on the children. Many children live in fear, uncertainty, and embarrassment. Addiction often becomes the family secret, and children are admonished to keep quiet. Children in homes where there is addictive behavior often risk their own lives to care for a parent or their own siblings. When we learn of these situations, we must do all in our power to help the family. Helping the addict find proper treatment is a big step toward recovery. Helping the family find support groups is essential.

The issue of bullying continues to plague our society as we increasingly learn and hear of it taking place at a younger and younger age. Bullying is no longer just a problem for teenagers; it is now affecting grade school and even preschool children. The victims of bullying live in constant fear and risk their lives each day when they are placed in situations where others inflict physical or emotional harm. The scars of bullying can remain with a child all of his or her life, unless he or she gets help. Adults should be on the alert for bullying situations inflicted on children and do all they can to alleviate the danger. They must be sensitive to children who face or have faced bullies in their lives. Adults can work toward boosting the self-esteem of these children.

Finally, there are children in many parts of the world who live in poverty and face life-threatening diseases. Other children are sent to fight wars and risk their lives for their nation. The reality, as hard as it is for adults to comprehend, is that many children face harsh, unpleasant childhoods. They risk their lives each day just to stay alive, and these children work hard just to find some sense of sanity in the worst life scenarios. Pray for these children each day. Give money to reputable organizations that work to alleviate poverty and childhood diseases or oppose sending children to war.

Just as David, in our biblical story, risked his life to save his nation, many children today risk their own lives. Some of these children merit recognition for heroic deeds. Others deserve praise and affirmation for living life in the midst of difficulties and perils many of us adults never face. The voice of David in our scripture is a constant reminder of a child's risk-taking efforts on behalf of his nation and his God. While we proclaim David as a true child hero, we also lift up the voices of other children who are risk-takers as well. And we cry out prayers of sorrow and hope for those children whose very survival depends on their taking risks that place them in grave and dangerous situations.

God faithfully walks beside these children each day. God holds risk-taking children in God's arms of grace and love. We adults are called to do the same.

QUESTIONS FOR REFLECTION AND DISCUSSION

1. Why do you think the story of David and Goliath is such a popular one with children?

2. Discuss how Saul imposes adult thinking and action on David's situation. How do we impose adult thinking on the risk-taking endeavors of children today?

3. Share some stories you have heard about children who have risked their lives for others and are heroes.

4. Do you personally know some children who have risked their lives to save others? Lift up their stories.

5. What are some of the large giants children face today?

6. What are some of the large giants you face in your own life?

7. What tools has God provided you with to fight the giants in your life?

8. Think of some risky situations you have found yourself in. How has God helped you?

9. Discuss some of the risky situations children face today.

10. How can the church reach out to children in risky and life-threatening situations and offer help to both children and their families?

A Child Cries Out

Read the Story: Genesis 21: 1–20

> *And God heard the voice of the boy; and the*
> *angel of God called to Hagar from heaven,*
> *and said to her, "What troubles you, Hagar?*
> *Do not be afraid; for God has heard the*
> *voice of the boy where he is."*
>
> Genesis 21:17 (NRSV)

Researchers at the University of Sussex studied the purring sounds of ten different cats. First, they recorded the cries of cats as they solicited food; then they recorded their cries in a different context. The research team recruited fifty people to rate the purrs on how pleasant or urgent they sounded. Consistently, the listeners rated the "solicitation purrs" as more demanding and certainly less pleasant than the other types of purrs. Apparently domestic cats emit a plaintive cry within their purrs, especially when they are hungry. Their unrelenting, insistent, and demanding purrs both irritate owners and appeal to their nurturing instincts. Cat owners could easily distinguish between the two kinds of purring.[3]

The cat cries mimicked the cries of babies! The team discovered this amazing fact when they examined the sound spectrum of the solicitation purrs and found an unusual peak, distinct from the frequencies of the usual purr. The solicitation purrs of the hungry or distressed cats contained a frequency range between 220–520 hertz, much higher than the purr range of cats that are content. When babies cry, the frequency range of their cries are similar to that of the needy cats, a range of 300–600 hertz.[4]

Cat owners admitted that they found the high-pitched meows hard to ignore, leading researchers to theorize that cats may exploit our human tendencies to respond to their cry-like sounds similar to that of human babies, just as we would respond to the cries of hungry infants. Research seems to indicate that cat owners find it just as difficult to ignore the cries of their felines as it is for parents to ignore the cries of their babies.[5]

In the story of Hagar and Ishmael, God found it impossible to ignore the cries of the infant child. In keeping with God's nature of compassion and love for all of God's children, God responded to Ishmael's hunger cries, much as a caring parent responds to the cries of his infant or perhaps as a caring cat owner responds to the cries of his "baby." Yet God fulfilled the parenting role in such a superior manner, outshining even the devoted and doting parent, and certainly ranking far above the most dedicated and often coerced cat owner. And while God never intended to neglect the sobs of Hagar, the mother of Ishamel, the angel of the Lord made it clear that God centered in on the cries of her helpless child. God's ears are particularly attuned to the cries of innocent, suffering children.

In answering the cries of Hagar's child, God answered her pleadings as well. Hagar sobbed, not for her own dilemma, but only for the welfare of her son. When God responded to Ishmael's cries, God also responded to Hagar's tears.

A review of the story helps us to understand the dire situation forced upon Hagar and her child. God promised childless Abraham and Sarah a descendant. When Sarah failed to get pregnant on her own time schedule, she grew tired of waiting and decided to take matters into her own hands. She insisted that Abraham sleep with Hagar, her maid. Hagar conceived and gave birth to Ishmael. When God blessed Sarah with the child Isaac, Sarah again took matters into her own hands. She demanded that Abraham banish Hagar and Ishmael into the stark and dangerous desert. Abraham reluctantly followed Sarah's wishes, leaving the woman and child in the desert with scarcity of food and water, which both soon ran out.

Imagine the distress of this mother when she realized that there was absolutely nothing she could do for her child. It became obvious to her that he faced a harsh impending death. Hagar placed her child under a bush to protect him from the sun, doing what she believed to be her last caring action as a mother. She refused to watch him die, so she removed herself a distance from the bush and began to sob. At the same time, her hungry and thirsty child began to wail.

An angel informed Hagar that God heard the cries of her son and the angel instructed her to hold her child's hand and lift the boy up. The angel further informed her that God intended to mold Ishmael into a leader of his own nation, just as God planned to form Isaac into a leader for the Jewish nation. God balanced Ishmael's leadership with Isaac's. God favored equality over injustice. God refused to play favorites and loved both sons of Abraham with equal passion.

When helpless Ishmael cried out, God responded. When desperate Hagar obeyed the angel, her eyes were opened. Her new and enlarged vision allowed her to spot a well of water. The well, already present in the desert, was hidden to Hagar in her state of hopelessness. Hagar failed to see her lifesaving channel of hope and renewal because of her tears and distress. Ishmael's voice, the crying voice of an infant, set into motion deliverance for them both. God heard the wailing voice of the crying child as it loudly rang out in the desert, pleading for deliverance. The distress call of Ishmael pierced the heart of God, and God sent deliverance.

The story focuses primarily on the cries of Ishmael, but also on his rejection. God understood the rejection of Ishmael and was sensitive to the burden and embarrassment this rejection placed upon Hagar. Ishmael and Hagar were ostracized from the household of Abraham and forced into the desert. Sarah's anger and jealousy greatly affected the life of an innocent child. God overturned anger and jealousy in favor of new opportunities for growth. The wilderness of the desert, a barren and foreboding landscape was transformed into an oasis of promise. New life burst forth in the midst of what once appeared to be a bleak and dismal scenario. God offered the child an affirming future rather than a cruel death.

This poignant biblical story provides us many lessons today as we deal with children and face distressing situations in our lives. The story admonishes us to listen carefully to the cries of children. God does and so must we. God hears the sad voices of neglected and abused children in our society today. God hears their passionate voices as they seek to share with us about their own hopes and fears. God hears their forceful and compelling voices as they work to articulate their faith and their dreams. God listens to the distressed voices of the children of the world as they cry out in the barren wilderness of poverty, war, bullying, and genocide. God hears, but also compels us to listen to these children's voices and respond. God calls us to work to alleviate the suffering we find behind the haunting voices of children. God never neglects the voices of hurting children, but sends us to respond, like God sent the angel to Hagar. God empowers us with the ability to take action against suffering. God uses us as messengers of hope and healing.

Sometimes, similar to the way Sarah felt about her son Isaac, we find ourselves favoring some children and ostracizing others. We want God to bless only the children we think are deserving of God's favor and grace. However, God loves all of the children of the world, regardless of their status, circumstance, nationality, or religious background. Understanding this behooves us to work to make changes for the betterment of children worldwide and in our own communities. Speaking out for justice for all God's children, rather than a select few, aligns us with God's call for righteousness. God hears our cries for justice, but expects us to work toward the alleviation of inequity and injustice.

The biblical passage compels us to consider ways we have cast out people or children because they are different than us. We all admit that there are times we have treated a child with AIDS, a child who has been left an orphan, a child who looks different, a child who is poor, or even a child who is not our own like an outcast. We must examine our hearts and consider the ways, like Sarah, we have rejected or banished a child to the wilderness because he or she failed to look like us, dress like us, talk like us, or worship like us.

God calls us to join hands with children and lift them up rather than distance ourselves from them. Our story informs us that Hagar distanced herself from her child, a bowshot distance of about one hundred yards. We must never distance ourselves from children; rather, we must take their hands in ours, lifting children up so that they can recognize their gifts and their full potential. Our affirming actions toward children can yield positive results as we seek to offer life-giving grace. Our concerns may ease and, in some cases, alleviate the stress of whatever burdens children face in the present. Our caring actions may provide children with much-needed confidence and enduring strength for the future. Children desire to have adults who confirm their gifts and encourage them. We bring hope to children when we encourage them rather than criticize them.

Like Ishmael, the children we encounter must be led to recognize that they have a wonderful inheritance in their faith, a God-given inheritance. The source of this gift comes from a loving God. The marvelous, God-given gift of inheritance in the faith is one which children should be taught to receive graciously and with thanksgiving. We are all children of God and heirs of God's good gifts. Adults share the teachings and principles of their faith tradition, passed down from generation to generation. Children understand the powerful significance of being a part of a faith community and growing in their faith. Involved adults help form, shape, and mold the faith of children. They teach children what it means to be a child of God. They model for children righteous living. They gladly avail themselves of the vital task of becoming faith mentors. These adults take the hands of children, lift them up, and endeavor to be positive role models in contrast to some adults who sadly distance themselves from children.

Just as God heard the cry of Ishmael in our biblical story, God hears our own cries of distress. Often God provides a well of relief, healing, and salvation for us, but we fail to see it because of our own tears of self-pity and our despondent feelings of hopelessness. However, God remains faithful to us in the situations we face in life, just as God remained present with Hagar and Ishmael. God is always a constant, abiding presence in the wilderness of our lives. We never know how God may answer our cries for help. Our transforming wells of help and hope may come through people God sends our way or messages we receive through sermons, prayers, well wishes, songs, devotional readings, or scripture passages. God provides an oasis, an overflowing spring of grace and peace in the midst of our deserts of life.

Perhaps, like Hagar, we plea to God for mercy and justice. We are concerned for those who have been cast out by society. Our convictions spill forth from our lips as we plea to God to do something to alleviate suffering and injustice. We cry out to God to help the neglected, the abused, the have-nots of this world. While God always hears our wails, God also expects us to partner with our Creator rather than sit back and complain. God urges us to speak out, take action, and use all available resources to alleviate suffering. We are to work earnestly to bring about God's kingdom upon this earth. God provides wells of nourishment and springs of living water when we work with God to offer hope to others. God responds to our cries for mercy when we provide others with wells of compassion and grace that flow from our faithful convictions as blessed children of God.

Our scripture assures us that God has a great purpose for all of us and a great inheritance for each person. God offered Ishmael a wonderful inheritance, and God offers each of us the same. God's intentions toward us are always good. Even when others reject us, ostracize us, hurt us, or abandon us, God remains faithful. God brings good out of the most difficult and challenging circumstances of our lives. God intends for us to enjoy as great a future as God planned for Ishmael. God knows our needs, our desires, and our future hopes. God brings valuable people into our lives: dedicated, caring, wise, and compassionate individuals who can help shape our destiny. Just as Hagar listened to the voice of the angel, we must attune our ears to their leadership and follow their guidance. These God-sent individuals often represent wells of hope for us in the midst of the hopeless and uncertain deserts we find ourselves thrust into. Often, wells of goodness and opportunity surround us, but like Hagar, we fail to see them because we are so caught up in our own distress. At such times, we need God to open our eyes and give us a clear vision of hope.

Sarah viewed this story as one about God blessing her child and her child only. Yet God rewrote the story and transformed it into one of promise and blessing for both children. In the same way, God rewrites our stories. Into the barren desert of our lives, God sends an angel of mercy to share with us the good news. We are not forgotten or abandoned. We are not left to die, thirsting for the water of redemption. We are not ostracized or neglected. Rather, we are remembered. God finds us where we are, seeks us out in the desert of our lives, and hears our parched and thirsty cries for mercy.

We discover, like Ishmael, that we are beloved children of God. Our inheritance, like Isaac's, is far greater than the countless stars in the nighttime sky. Our inheritance, like Ishmael's, numbers far greater than the countless sands in the barren desert. And like Hagar, just when we need it, God provides a well, springing forth with waters of mercy, grace, compassion, and love. We drink from it gladly, for it offers us true salvation.

The question is whether we have the eyes of faith to see our deliverance even in the midst of our tears. So often, we are no different from Hagar; our tears sometimes blind us to the wells of God's nourishing love and mercy. They blind us, that is, until God sends us our own messenger of hope. We never know whom God will send, however. Sometimes our messenger could be an angel, but often that person is a wise family member, a devoted friend, or a trusted pastor. Also, God sends the Holy Spirit to teach us, strengthen us, and guide us. When the messenger appears, we will know that he or she has been sent from God to rescue us from our own deserts of despair. Thus, when the messenger speaks, it is important for us to both listen and obey, just as Hagar listened and obeyed the angel of the Lord.

With trust and confidence in our amazing God, we should dry our tears, look into the distance, and see the well of God's salvation. When we drink deeply from its life-giving waters, we discover, like Hagar and Ishmael did, that God offers us an everlasting inheritance as sons and daughters of our Father, God.

Questions For Reflection And Discussion

1. What are the reasons some children are crying out in your faith community and in the communities in which you live? What actions can you, your community, or the church take to alleviate their suffering?

2. What are the reasons some children are crying out in our world today? What can you, your church, or society do to alleviate some of the suffering of children in the world today?

3. Discuss the hopeless situation of Hagar and Ishmael. Can you relate their story to any circumstances in your own life? If you feel comfortable, share that experience. Talk about the ways in which you experienced God working for good during that time.

4. Do you think that the well Hagar eventually saw was already present in the desert? Discuss why you believe this to be true or false. If you believe the well was already present in the desert, discuss why you think Hagar was unable to see it?

5. In what ways have you distanced yourself from children and why?

6. How can you join hands with children today? How can you lift up the children you come in contact with in your own life?

7. Be honest in sharing ways you have cast out children. Why did you cast out or look unfavorably on these children? Describe these children. Discuss your fears, anxieties, and reasons for the actions and thoughts you had toward the children. Take time to offer to God a prayer of repentance.

8. How can you and the church help children understand their wonderful inheritance in the Lord?

9. In what ways are you hurting today? In what ways have you seen God respond to your hurt by offering you wells of healing? What person has God sent into your life that represented to you the angel of the Lord? How did this person alleviate your fear or help you in your time of need? Offer a prayer of thanks for this person.

10. How is God rewriting the past story of your life and shaping it into a new story of love and grace?

A Child Trusts His Father

Read the Story: Genesis 22: 1–17

> *Isaac said to his father, "The fire and the wood are here, but where is the lamb for a burnt offering?"*
>
> Genesis 22:7 (NRSV)

Seven-year-old Will Hurt places unwavering trust in his father. His loyalty and devotion toward his father, Scott, are obvious to all who know the two. Will shadows his father wherever he goes. One views the steady picture of the father, a giant of a man, walking next to the small boy. Will constantly strives to follow in Scott's fatherly footsteps and proudly seeks to emulate his lifestyle.

One observed this at church, when, at the age of four, Will decided he wanted to usher alongside his father. So, down the aisle he marched, uninhibited, undeterred, determined to stand tall beside his dad and the other ushers. Son and father, tutor and the one being tutored. week after week Will demonstrated that he had what it took to become the youngest usher in the history of his congregation. He wanted to be an usher for one reason and one reason only: that was his dad's important role in the church, and he desired to be exactly like his dad. Will became an imitation of his father.

Will's father is currently employed as an emergency medical technician, stationed at the local fire station. From the time Will was a small child, he wished to follow in his father's footsteps. His favorite toys are his fire trucks, and he readily vocalizes that one day he will himself become a fire fighter or some occupation closely linked to his father's. Will shadows his father at church, at home, and everywhere they go. They share a strong bond of trust, love, and loyalty that seems unbreakable.

The biblical writer of the book of Genesis fails to tell us about the relationship between Isaac and his father, Abraham. Yet one cannot help but wonder if Abraham and Isaac forged a strong relationship of trust similar to Will and Scott. The text seems to indicate that Isaac willing and obediently followed his father and continued to do so even when he realized his father had brought no sacrifice for their altar. Isaac appears in the text as a very young boy. He showed perfect obedience toward his father. Too young to grasp the severity of the situation for himself, he exhibited childlike trust.

Isaac has only one line in the biblical narrative, but the answer to his one-line question ultimately determines the outcome of the story and reveals several important theological truths about God and God's relationship with mankind. His only line in the biblical narrative was one he uttered with complete and ultimate trust. Isaac question proves to be the same question the reader poses for himself. The answer to his poignant and provocative question reveals much about God and God's destiny for the nation of Israel. Isaac posed a question that demanded an answer, and the answer was soon revealed when God offered a ram as a sacrifice rather than a boy. We need to hear Isaac's trusting voice as it teaches us about what God demands of us today.

This text challenges our faith. It forces us to address questions about God and God's nature. Did God desire Abraham to sacrifice Isaac in order to show obedience toward God? Does God need that kind of ultimate loyalty from great leaders? Would God put Abraham in such a stressful, horrible situation, a position in which Abraham believed that he was going to lose his beloved offspring, his promise from God? Would God do that to Abraham, knowing that Isaac was the true hope for the continuance of future generations for Abraham? Would God allow this to happen to his faithful servant Abraham, knowing full well that, at the last minute, a sacrifice would be provided? Or perhaps had Abraham misunderstood God's call and purpose in this situation? We cannot hear with clarity the voice of young Isaac until we answer some of these difficult questions.

Let's first examine the cultural setting Abraham found himself living in. The culture surrounding Abraham practiced child sacrifice and did so without apology, regret, or remorse. The firstborn male was placed on a fire and sacrificed to the fertility god Baal. Baal's followers believed the god would bless them with more children if they were loyal to him. When Abraham set out to sacrifice his son, Isaac, his firstborn, he caved in to the pressures and demands of the culture around him. His understanding of God's call got shifted from one of *dedication* of the firstborn to *sacrifice* of the firstborn. The book of Leviticus teaches that firstborn sons are not to be "passed through the fire," a reference to child sacrifice, but rather are to be dedicated to God. This teaching is reiterated in Deuteronomy 18: 9–10a (NRSV): "When you come into the land that the Lord your God is giving you, you must not learn to imitate the abhorrent practices of those nations. No one shall be found among you who makes a son or daughter pass through fire."

Either Abraham misunderstood God's call or he reshaped God's call. God never intended Abraham to practice child sacrifice. Rather, God's plan depended on Abraham dedicating Isaac. When Abraham completely misunderstood, God stepped in and provided a sacrifice of a ram. Yet the biblical text allows us to see Abraham's flaws as he struggled with God's call versus the pressures of the culture he lived in. The biblical narrative honestly addresses the growing understanding of this great leader as he changed in his perspective of God and God's dealings with him and his nation. The Bible allows us to grasp the emerging theology of God's people as this God-talk was shaped and formed by events such as the Abraham and Isaac story.

When Isaac called out to his father with his question, we hear his voice as that of all children who cry out for justice. Isaac's question reminds us that children are precious to God. God values the life of each child. God holds each child in high esteem. Abraham lived surrounded by a society that devalued children and took their lives without a mere thought. The Canaanites worshiped a god who demanded the sacrifice of firstborn sons in order to assure many children. Abraham worshiped a God who asked that the firstborn son be dedicated, not sacrificed. So we affirm the voice of young Isaac, a voice that reminds us of trust in a father, Abraham, and also trust in a heavenly Father. We also hear his voice as a reminder for us to examine closely our call from God. Each of us must closely examine our own call to see if we are being led in the right direction or being swayed by the forces of our culture.

Isaac's voice teaches us to remember in our own time and culture that children are valuable. They are not worthless commodities to be thrown away or treated as second-class citizens. As God's people, we grieve over the exploitation of children. Children face mental and physical abuse, child labor, child slave labor, poverty, diseases, malnutrition, bullying, and other forms of violation and neglect. We must advocate for the rights of children throughout the world. We must never neglect to love and praise the children in our care. Each child deserves to be viewed as a worthy child of God. Children will never know the love of God toward them unless we, as adults, demonstrate that love. Parents can dedicate all of their children to God and let each child know how much they are deemed worthy by the parents and others who have contact with them.

The biblical story of Abraham and Isaac also probes us to examine carefully our own call from God. Sometimes we, like Abraham, shape the call of God and mold it into our own desire. We, like Abraham, are often influenced by the culture around us. We sometimes give into peer pressure. We hear the enticing voices of the culture, luring us into thinking that what we are doing is God's will, when in reality, it is just the opposite. We can be so persuaded that the action we are taking is God's direction for our life, when it may be the culture putting pressure on us to act in a certain way or follow a false guide.

Abraham and his nation eventually came to understand that God did not desire child sacrifice, but child dedication. Often God has to clarify our own calls for us. This requires us to be open to listening and discerning. Trusted friends and mentors often help us more fully understand God's call, just as Isaac's questioning voice perhaps helped Abraham to recognize that God did not intend Isaac to be given up as a sacrifice. Scripture helps us more fully process God's call, both confirming that call and leading us into greater paths of service. Sometimes we find that we are headed in the wrong direction, and we must turn around and find peace and comfort in seeking God's call in a new, exciting manner.

Perhaps what bothers us most in our passage of scripture is the interpretation often heard, preached, and taught that God needed Abraham to be obedient so that God could make him into a great leader. Therefore, God tested Abraham. Most of us believers have difficulty with a God who asked Abraham to blindly obey, knowing all along that God planned to rescue Abraham at the last minute. Obviously, God wanted Abraham to be obedient, as that is God's desire for each of us. However, we do not serve a God who plays tricks on us at the last minute. We serve a God who understands that we sometimes get our actions and motives wrong, very wrong, and end up in complicated situations. Then, God offers us a way out just as God provided for Abraham. Abraham misunderstood God's intentions, but God brought good out of what could have resulted in a disastrous situation for both Isaac and Abraham.

We recall that God blessed Abraham and promised to make his heirs like the stars in the night sky. Why would God turn around and obliterate that promise by having Abraham sacrifice his only heir? Abraham was the one who almost destroyed his own legacy by his misdirected actions. God was the one who continued the promise to Abraham by providing a ram rather than letting Abraham sacrifice his son. God offered justice for Isaac and kept the promise of future generations alive in the heart of Abraham.

Will Hurt trusts his father, Scott. Isaac trusted his father, Abraham. Whenever one hears Will Hurt speak of his father, he speaks with the voice that demands to be heard. He tells others that his father is good, kind, loving, strong, and worthy of emulation. When we hear the voice of Isaac in our biblical passage, his too is a voice that demands to be heard. He speaks for all children who question adults. He asks if we really care, if we really believe that children are good and worthwhile. He asks us if we love children enough to dedicate them to the Lord rather than abuse and neglect them. Yet even above the clear voice of

Will and above the questioning voice of Isaac, we hear another voice. God's voice demands to be heard also. God's voice comes with a call to each of us. Then God comes bringing the very gift we need to rework and reshape that call until we get it just right. For Abraham, it was a ram. Who knows what it will be for each of us?

Questions For Reflection And Discussion

1. What difficulties do you have with the biblical story of Abraham and Isaac? In what ways does the story test your theological thinking about God?

2. Think of children you know who place ultimate trust in their parents, pastors, friends, and church leaders. Discuss ways you can assure children that you are trustworthy.

3. How have you understood God's call in your own life? In what ways have you tried to reshape God's call to fit your own purposes and desires? How do you discover God's call today? What tools does God provide?

4. Name some of the ways you caved into the pressures and demands of the culture around you. In what ways do you see churches giving in to the pressures and demands of the culture around them?

5. How can the church teach parents and children skills to help them avoid giving in to the pressures and demands of the culture?

6. How does your church dedicate children to the Lord? Do you have a ceremony of baptism or dedication?

7. Name some ways you show children that they are valuable to you and your congregation.

8. Discuss in what ways society devalues children.

9. Think of a time in which you found yourself in a risky, bad, or troubling situation. How did God help you?

10. Does your church support or lead any ceremonies that offer affirmation to children? If so, discuss these ceremonies, and share ways in which they affirm children.

A Child Hears God Call

Read the Story: I Samuel 3: 1–19

> *Now the Lord came and stood there, calling*
> *as before, "Samuel, Samuel!"And Samuel*
> *said, "Speak, for your servant is listening."*
>
> I Samuel 3:10 (NRSV)

Sixth grader Jessica Mink woke up in the middle of the night, and sleep eluded her. She thought about the homeless in her community who did not have comfortable beds on which to rest their tired bodies or warm clothes to wear that would shelter them from the harsh cold of the soon-approaching winter. In her restlessness, God called Jessica to take action. He planted a dream in the heart of this child. God gave her a vision of her congregation gathering bundles of winter coats, mittens, hats, and gloves and then delivering them to the homeless. Jessica believed God wanted her to spearhead the efforts of her church. God inspired Jessica with a plan to help others, but God also awakened in Jessica the desire to lead others in order to make her vision a reality.

Jessica shared her plan with her parents, who advised her to talk with her pastors. When Jessica sat down with her pastors, they were very supportive of her idea and gave her their full approval. They encouraged her to share her vision with the entire congregation and enlist the help of the youth in her congregation.

Jessica took her call from God seriously. She sprang into action. One Sunday morning, she stood up in front of her congregation and made an adamant plea for coats and warm clothing for the homeless. She presented statistics about homelessness in her community. Furthermore, she encouraged the congregation not to just gather warm clothes, but to also reach out and become active in the delivery of the gifts. She promised training to all who wished to become involved. She decorated boxes and placed them at strategic areas throughout the church building. Soon, all of her boxes were overflowing with coats, hats, mittens, and gloves.

Jessica then contacted a pastor in her community who worked directly with the homeless. He met with those volunteers who wished to distribute the clothing and offered them training in dealing with homeless people. One afternoon, the volunteers gathered at the church, prayed together, and then went to the area where the homeless awaited them. They distributed the warm clothing and passed out food, smiles, and encouraging words to the homeless. To think this wonderful outreach all started when a child heard God call in the night and responded to God's challenge.

Like Jessica, young Samuel heard God call in the night. Samuel lived at the temple with Eli, the priest. He arrived at the temple when he was three years of age. His mother, Hannah, who has been barren until the birth of Samuel, promised God that if God blessed her with an heir, she would present that child to God. Samuel served in God's house, assisting the priest with his duties.

One night, as he slept, he heard a voice calling his name. Samuel thought the priest, Eli, was calling him, but Eli denied this. After the third time interrupting Eli's sleep, Eli advised Samuel that God might be calling him, so he was to listen and respond. Samuel obeyed his mentor. Samuel listened, God called, and Samuel responded. Samuel understood the serious nature of his call once God revealed it to him. God wanted him to address the disobedience of the evil sons of Eli. This call required him to speak challenging and forceful words to the sons of Eli, but it also put him in an uncomfortable position. He knew that his call directly affected his teacher and spiritual adviser. This worried Samuel, and he was afraid to tell Eli about his call from God.

Initially, Samuel hid the details of his prophetic call as he wished to shelter Eli and not hurt his feelings. However, Eli demanded that Samuel share God's words with him. The revelation as hard as it was for

Eli to hear, met with the priest's approval. Eli agreed that Samuel must obey God and speak the truth. Samuel continued to serve in the temple with Eli until the time he assumed his duties as a prophet of God.

Eli the priest mentored Samuel. He helped him discover and recognize God's call in his life. He encouraged Samuel to fulfill that call, no matter where it might lead him. Eli understood that this was Samuel's destiny in life, and he offered his full support, regardless of how much the prophetic words impacted his own family.

The voice of the child Samuel leaps forth from the pages of scripture and impacts us even today. His voice is both strong and submissive. The story stands as a powerful one for both children and adults to read and appreciate. The story involves a child who was called by God for a serious task as a prophet, a spokesperson for God. Samuel's words would make a great difference in the nation of Israel. His words would impact others and lead his people in the right direction. God challenged Samuel to speak out against the injustices of the sons of Eli. God asked a child to prepare for a future where he would have to address the evil and unrighteous actions of the sons of his mentor. Surely Samuel felt humbled to be called by God at such an early age and asked to perform the momentous task that God told him to do.

When Samuel finally understood who was calling him, that made all the difference in the world. Samuel was unsure until Eli clarified the situation for him. Samuel viewed Eli as a trusted guide and teacher. So when he adviseed Samuel to be quiet and listen, Samuel obeyed. When he informed Samuel that perhaps God was calling him, Samuel anticipated the call. So when God called Samuel by name, there was no hesitation on the child's part. He eagerly awaited a word from God. He willingly answered, "Speak, for your servant is listening." In his words and his actions, Samuel models for each of us the way we should respond when God calls us.

The text offers us several guidelines for the way we should respond to God's call in each of our lives. First, God called Samuel by name. This assures us that God knows each of us by name and uses our names to call us to important tasks. One of the most moving passages in scripture involving the use of a name occurred when Jesus called Mary

Magdalene by name. This incident took place after Jesus' resurrection, when Mary and Jesus encountered each other in a garden. There, Mary failed to recognize Jesus until he called her name.

Our names identify us. Most of us value our names and place importance on others knowing them. One of the most embarrassing social blunders is to call someone by the wrong name. Children especially deem it important for others to remember their names. When friends, teachers, and pastors call children by their names, this speaks volumes to the children. This lets them know they are special to the individual who takes the time to remember their names and then uses them in conversation. Samuel felt special to God when God called him using his name rather than just "child" or "boy." In the same way, we know that God calls us using our names. Our names identify each of us as a special child of God. God believes we are worthy of having our names called out, so God addresses us by name.

At first, Samuel was unsure who was calling him. This happens to all of us from time to time. Eli's role in our story becomes extremely important. Eli helped Samuel discern the voice of God above other voices. We all need mentors in our lives who can help us determine whether the visions we receive for ministry and outreach are from God or others. Our earnest efforts at serving can often be stifled and unsuccessful if their origins do not come from God, but from the culture around us. Often we mistake the false voices of our world as the true voice of God, when they are anything but the voice of God. It helps to turn to trusted friends and mentors and seek their advice before we proceed. Jessica did this when she turned to her family and pastor to verify her call. Samuel did this when he turned to Eli for help. Perhaps children are often more willing to do this than adults. They do not have our reluctance to seek the guidance and knowledge of others. We do well to commend Samuel for his eagerness to turn to his mentor, and we do well to emulate his actions.

Samuel listened. Samuel heard. How often do we listen to God, truly listen? Amid the noise of our world, we often tune out God. God speaks to us in many ways. Sometimes God speaks through a poem or song, others times through a sermon. Many times, God speaks to us through the advice of a trusted friend or family member. Other times, God uses prayer, meditation, or the scriptures. Samuel teaches us the importance of truly listening and not talking.

We cannot hear God unless we quiet ourselves. Before we can respond to God, we must listen to know what God wants to tell us. Many of us complain that God never calls us to do anything important. Perhaps God calls us, but we are too busy talking so we fail to hear. We are too busy telling God what to do or moving ahead of God, taking matters into our own hands, and we squash the voice of God. Our loud voices drown out God's call. Take time, like Samuel, to be still and listen. Quiet yourself, remove the noise from your life, and listen for God to call you by name.

Both Jessica Mink and Samuel listened to God and then responded. Jessica busied herself with reaching out to the homeless. Samuel began to prepare himself to become a prophet of the Lord. These children teach us that it does no good to listen to God and then fail to respond. Jessica and Samuel also wisely admitted their fears. Jessica related to her pastors that speaking in front of her congregation filled her with anxiety. She promised to speak, however, for she comprehended that sharing with others about her vision was essential in garnering support for her project. Samuel feared that his harsh words, when delivered to the sons of Eli, would put him in grave danger. However, he overcame his apprehension with the knowledge that God guided and directed his life. God's call often places us in uncomfortable positions and leads us to places where we would rather not go. Yet, like Jessica and Samuel, we too must accept our calling to be on a mission for God. We must not shrink away from God's purpose for each of us. We should gladly and joyfully accept our call to be God's people and serve God in whatever way we are asked. For like Jessica and Samuel, we too know that God faithfully walks beside us and direct our efforts with God's loving grace and constant care.

God never calls us to impossible tasks. God never expects us to act alone. Jessica recruited her entire congregation. Samuel turned to his friend Eli. God provides us the tools and resources to carry out His purpose for us. Jessica used her gifts of organization and her leadership skills to inspire her congregation to take action. God honed Samuel's prophetic skills under the tutelage of Eli the priest. In a time of need, God always provides just the right people and opens exactly the right doors so that we can fulfill our calling in precisely the right way, the way that pleases and honors God.

QUESTIONS FOR REFLECTION AND DISCUSSION

1. Do you know any children in your congregation or community who have taken the lead in recruiting adults and others for a worthwhile outreach project? Share their story.

2. How can churches take steps to alleviate poverty or help the homeless in the community?

3. In what ways can adults mentor children? How have you been a mentor to children?

4. How has the call of God placed you in an uncomfortable position?

5. Why are our names important? How do you learn the names of the children in your congregation or community? Why is it important to know the names of children?

6. How do you quiet yourself and listen for God's call in your life?

7. How can you discern whether God is calling you to a particular task?

8. In what ways does the culture around you try to block out God's call in your life?

9. What lessons can we teach children that will help produce in them good listening skills? Discuss some ways of teaching that might be effective for children today.

10. Name some of the mission projects the children in your congregation have organized and led.

A Child Serves As King

Read the Story: 2 Kings 11–12

> *Jehoash did what was right in the sight of the
> Lord all his days, because the priest Jehoiada
> instructed him.*
>
> 2 Kings 12: 2 (NRSV)

Pharaoh Tutankhamun ascended to the throne at nine or ten years
of age. Most historians believe that Tutankhamun had very powerful
advisors to help him, including General Horemheb and Maya, the
overseer of the treasury. Reports inform us that General Horemheb had
the ability to calm the young king when his temper flared.[6]

Although young in age, Pharaoh Tutankhamum reversed several
edicts made by his father during his reign, some of which made for a
stronger nation. He restored the god Amun to supremacy in Egypt,
rejecting the worship of the god Aten. The pharaoh decided that the
capital city would no longer be located in Akhetaten, but in Thebes. The
king initiated elaborate building projects and reinstated the traditional
festivals of the land. Tutankhamun inherited a weak economy and
sought to boost diplomatic relations with other kingdoms.[7]

Second Kings records the story of Jehoash, who began his reign,
like Pharoah Tutankhamun, at an early age. At the age of seven years,
Jehoash became the eighth ruler of the southern kingdom of Judah.
However, his journey to the throne turned out to be a difficult and
dangerous one. One of his relatives, Athaliah, wished to destroy the
royal family. She immediately usurped power and took over the reins

of the kingdom. Unpopular Athaliah ruled for six years. Athaliah ordered a massacre of all individuals who opposed her. During this time, Jehoash's aunt Jehosheba looked out for the well-being of the future king. She hid him, thus saving him from the massacre commanded by Athaliah. Jehoash remained the only surviving male descent of his grandfather, Jerhoram. When the time was right, his great-uncle, the high priest Jehoiada, crowned and anointed him king at the young age of seven. Although Athaliah greatly protested, she was stripped of her royal powers and put to death.[8]

Like Pharaoh Tutankhamun, who had wise advisors to instruct him, Jehoash relied on his great uncle, the high priest Jerhoram. As long as the high priest lived, the scriptures tell us that Jehoash pleased God with his actions as the ruler of the kingdom of Judah. He favored the worship of God and observed the Law. Jehoash set out to repair the house of the Lord, which fell into disarray during the reign of Athaliah. He sent the priests of his kingdom, the Levites, throughout the country to collect money for repairs to the temple. However, when the process of collecting money and repairing the temple took too long, Jehoash ordered a collection box placed at the temple where worshippers might deposit their money. After the people deposited many coins in the box, Jehoash gave them to the carpenters, mason, and workmen, who repaired the house of the Lord.[9]

Jehoash reigned for forty years. Unfortunately, after the death of his mentor, the high priest Jerhoram, Jehoash strayed from the worship of God and began to support other gods besides Yahweh. When the Syrian King Hazael led his armies toward Jerusalem and marched against the city, Jehoash bribed the king with gold from the royal and sacred treasuries. The bribes worked, and Hazael turned back toward his own country, leaving Judah in peace. Jehoash ended up being assassinated by one of his own servants.[10]

Second Kings provides us with the interesting voice of a young king. Initially his voice rang out for what was right, good, and pleasing to God. Eventually, however, we hear his voice change for the worse. What once was a strong cry for justice and righteousness became a shaky voice for wrong thinking and inept action. His voice evolved into one that condoned bribery and foolishness. Where once he called out to the true God of Israel, now his voice shifted and he called out to false gods. He forsook the true God and pledged his allegiance to the god Baal. The culture shaped him and enticed him to forget his religious upbringing in favor of power and greed. He led his people down a wrong path of destruction, injustice, and evil. He ignored the advice of his faithful mentor and pursued his own twisted path, which led him astray. He forgot that God demanded that rulers display leadership above reproach.

What can his voice teach us today, especially as we relate to children? First, God calls children for important tasks. God endows children with the ability to lead. Think about the children you know who daily assume leadership roles in the church, their school, and their community. These children possess amazing God-given gifts similar to those Jehoash possessed. His mentor and the kingdom of Judah permitted Jehoash to use his gifts. They recognized his authority even when he was a young boy. Adults must affirm the gifts of children and allow them to serve in leadership roles along with adult assistance. Many children today yearn to use their gifts in service to others. They need adults who will step up, recognize the gifts of children, help mold and strengthen these gifts, and set children free to use their gifts in a variety of ways and places. The community, schools, and churches become more vital institutions when children use their gifts in service to others.

Just as the high priest mentors Jehoash in our Bible story, children desperately desire and need dedicated, godly mentors who show interest in their well-being. As long as Jehoash heeded the instructions of his mentor he pleased God with his words and actions. Good, kind mentors influence children to do what is right. They encourage children to reach out to others and show love and compassion. They guide children in the right directions, giving them moral and religious instruction. It behooves children to listen to their elders, parents, friends, pastors, teachers, and mentors and not reject their teaching, as did Jehoash. One hopes that strong mentors can yield a powerful influence on children, one that remains with them through their lifetime. One never knows the outcome, however. All adults can do is to plant good seeds in the hearts and minds of children and hope they come to fruition in the lives of the children they seek to mentor. This is a sacred task and not one to be taken lightly.

As Jehoash served his kingdom with integrity, he led his people away from false gods and instructed them to worship the only true God. Eventually he faltered and turned away from Yahweh to worship other deities. Today we must be always alert to seek after God and not let the false gods of the culture around us lure us into their traps. These false gods have myriad faces, and we encounter them each day in our world. We name some of these gods as pride, greed, status, wealth, false religion, hatred, and prejudice. Following the leadership of those who diligently and rightly guide us toward the true God helps us keep on the right path in life. It is easy to be persuaded by voices that are not righteous and people who do not devote themselves to the teachings of God. Jehoash reminds us of how easy it is to be lead into bribery when one lives in fear and lets the threats of others intimidate us into false thinking.

On a positive note, Jehoash worked diligently to restore the destruction of God's house. Even though the task became arduous and time-consuming, he refused to give up hope. He kept on until he secured the money necessary to make the needed repairs. We can all learn a lesson on persistence from Jehoash. We also find that he invested his time in a valuable project. Repairing the house of the Lord proved to be a worthwhile endeavor. We can examine our own motives when we decide to invest our time in projects or what we perceive to be a worthy cause. We must make sure we put our time, effort, money, and energy in support of causes and projects that produce good and lasting results. We need to consider whether the process helps us grow into steady, mature people or hinders our growth as children of God. We must evaluate whether the outcome achieves results that please God, helps alleviate suffering, and produces positive change.

For too brief a time in the kingdom of Judah, a child's voice rang out clear and strong. The child's voice proclaimed words that pleased God. God listened as the child spoke with the voice of authority, competence, sanity, righteousness, and integrity. This ruler's people listened also, and his voice led them to accomplish what was good and just. Sadly, however, the adult voice eventually took over. The adult voice diminished and destroyed the child's voice. The adult voice uttered destructive words, insane words, and words that led a kingdom away from the teachings of God. The voice failed to honor God and lacked the power to lead followers in the right direction.

We pray that our children never abandon their good voices by replacing them with the voices of evil. We hope they never turn a deaf ear to the once influential voices in their lives and instead listen to the persuasive voices of the culture around them. We trust they never leave behind the reasonable voices of their childhood to listen to voices that harm them rather than lift them up. Our fervent longing as adult mentors for children is that they never shut out affirming voices that speak to them. Our desire is that they never claim as their own a harsh, oppressive voice, rather that they quickly turn away in favor of a peaceful, prophetic voice. Jehoash stands as an example of the ways children and adults sometimes forsake the powerful voices of instruction found in good mentors. We all know of such mentors who tried to help us in the past, whose voices we listened to at one point, but eventually forgot or neglected to follow.

We must carefully examine the voices that influence us today and guide and direct our children. Unless we conduct a thorough examination into our own lives and that of our children, like Jehoash, we too can be led astray. It is easy to be led down the wrong path when we allow wrong voices to overshadow good voices in our lives. With God's help, we can discern which voices we should follow and which we should neglect.

When we stop listening to the competent, grace-filled voices God sends our way, we could end up following in the same direction as Jehoash. The path he took only led to his own downfall and that of his people. How much better for him and his kingdom had he kept alive the passionate voice of his childhood and continued to speak to his people with words of conviction, honesty, and truth. In the same way, our lives turn out for the better when we use our voices in ways that please God. What a difference we can make in transforming our world when our voices lead others and us to righteous living.

Questions For Reflection And Discussion

1. In what ways does your congregation allow children to serve in leadership roles? Discuss ways you offer training to these children.

2. Who are some of the key children leaders in your congregation? Name them, and offer prayers of thanksgiving for these children.

3. Reflect on ways you have allowed the culture to shape you. In what ways have you forsaken your upbringing in the process?

4. Discuss the importance of children listening to the advice of trusted mentors.

5. Discuss ways in which your congregation takes care of your church building. Talk about ways you teach children respect for the sanctuary and ways to practice good stewardship of your church facilities.

6. Think of an example of a child who started out on the right path, but was led astray. Discuss ways to keep children on the right path in life.

7. Name some people who you believe speak with the voice of authority today.

8. What voices are not good voices for children to hear?

9. Discuss the places in the world where you believe that your church is speaking out with a clear voice. What message is your church conveying to the world?

10. Reflect on ways you are using your voice for justice and peace.

A Child Rules His Kingdom

Read the Story: 2 Kings 22 –23:30

> *He did what was right in the sight of the*
> *Lord, and walked in all the ways of his father*
> *David; he did not turn aside to the right or*
> *to the left.*
>
> 2 Kings 22:2 (NRSV)

The fourteenth Dalai Lama, Lhamo Dhondrub, was born to poor farmers in a small village in a region of Tibet. When the thirteenth Dalai Lama died, a search party, disguised as travelers, set out to find the new Dalai Lama. When Lhamo was only two years old, the search party arrived at his home and asked to rest there overnight. This was common practice, and it was bad luck for a family to deny travelers a place to sleep or food to eat. The search party left the next morning, but returned three weeks later to ask directions. Two weeks after this, the travelers returned to the home of Lhamo, for they sensed that they might be in the presence of the new Dalai Lama. On February 22, 1940, at the age of four, Lhamo Dhondrub was officially declared the Dalai Lama and enthroned. In 1989, he was awarded the Nobel Peace Prize for his consistent opposition to violence as a solution to international conflicts, human rights issues, and global environmental problems. He remained so strongly committed to non-violence that he stated he would resign his position as the spiritual leader of the Tibetan people if they ever staged violent protests against the Chinese.[11]

Second Kings records the story of a leader, like the Dalai Lama, who stood for what was right in his kingdom. Josiah began his reign over the kingdom of Judah at eight years of age and ruled for thirty-one years. While king, he instituted major reforms long overdue in his kingdom. Josiah arrived on the throne at just the right time to rescue his kingdom from unrighteous living. Prior to his coming to the throne, he followed in the footsteps of both his grandfather and father, whom the Bible characterizes as vicious and evil kings. Both refused to worship God and led the people in the worship of idols. His grandfather, Manasseh, practiced witchcraft, erected an idol in God's temple, sacrificed his son to an idol, and killed many innocent people. His father also worshiped idols and refused to walk in the way of the Lord. Josiah proved to be a very different king from both his father and grandfather. Josiah worked diligently to remove the false idols from the land and restore the true worship of Yahweh.[12]

When King Josiah became a young adult, he ordered the High Priest Hilkiah to use previously collected tax money to renovate the temple. When Hilkiah cleared and restored the treasure room of the temple, he found a scroll described as the book of the Law. King Josiah read the book, and it astonished him how far the people had strayed from God's laws and commandments. It distressed Josiah when he realized that the people have erred in their ways, and he recognized that they must return to God. Josiah called for a national revival. He demanded that the book containing God's commands be read to all of the people of his kingdom. Josiah outlawed all forms of worship except allegiance to Yahweh. He destroyed all pagan objects and anything associated with the false god Baal.[13]

Josiah also reinstituted the Passover celebrations of the Jewish people, traditions and customs that played a pivotal part in the history of the Jewish nation but which had not been observed for some time in his kingdom. He insisted that the people diligently observe Passover and instructed them in the correct way to worship and serve God. Passover had not been so carefully observed in the nation for hundreds of years until Josiah worked to bring dignity and honor to this sacred tradition.[14]

The Bible tells us that Josiah followed in the footsteps of his ancestor David, a king whom the people respected and revered. Scripture commends Josiah for doing what is right. He faced a past scarred by the evil deeds of his grandfather and father, but he refused to allow the past to shape his future. He rejected the sins of his grandfather and father, and in so doing broke the chain that bound him and his people to the past. He bravely recounted the lawless errors of his subjects but sought to plant them firmly on a good path for the future. He decided that the past would not define his reign. He brought forth sweeping reforms because he renounced the misdeeds that kept him from serving God. He shunned the mistakes of his ancestors. He showed remorse for the sins of the past. He knew that his nation was headed in the wrong direction. He advised the people to repent and follow God's laws. He commited himself to change. He guided his people in a new direction. He turned his heart toward God, respected the Word of God, depended on God for guidance, and showed honor for the sacred traditions of his people.[15]

We hear the voice of Josiah in our present time as he speaks out for what is just and right. Many of us live with past sins and regrets that bind us. Josiah's voice frees us to move forward. Josiah encourages us to leave behind whatever chains us to the past. He admonishes us to let God remove any obstacles that we continue to cling to that only keep us shackled and broken. These barriers keep us from faithfully serving God. God provides Josiah with the strength and courage to let go of the past, and God does the same for us today. Just think of all Josiah had to overcome. Both his father and his grandfather could have yielded great influence on Josiah, but he decided to break the cycle of abuse and injustice his predecessors imposed on the people. He vowed to rule with righteousness and integrity.

Josiah proved that God endows children with wisdom. Although his reform came when he was a young adult, surely God placed in Josiah's heart the need for change at an early age. God worked to form Josiah into a leader of integrity. God provided Josiah with the resources, the strength, and the right individuals to help carry out his reforms. Many children today seek to be of service to God and bring about productive changes in their schools, churches, and communities. Adults need to encourage these children to use their wisdom to make a difference. Sometimes adults neglect to recognize the wisdom that children possess, so they ignore the voices of children when these children speak wise words. However, Josiah proved that God grants wisdom to children, and their pivotal, passionate voices can make our difference in our world today.

Josiah demonstrated a teachable spirit. Although he served as king, he listened to the high priest when he revealed to Josiah the discovery of God's Law. Josiah used his skills as king and student to probe further into the ancient text. In them, he recognized the value of their lessons and gain clarity on the importance of sharing God's Word with all his people. He sought to strengthen the nation and turned to the ideals and traditions in the history of his nation. Rather than make up his own laws, he yielded to a higher authority found in scripture. We all know children like Josiah whom God empowers with teachable spirits. These children are a blessing to others, and their teachable spirits need to be shaped by biblical truths and values.

Josiah teaches us of the importance of the traditions of our faith. Teaching children the traditions of their own communities of faith offers them the opportunity to participate in important rituals. Children enjoy using their senses in learning, and the celebrations of their faith provide opportunities for participation in hands-on learning. When children are allowed and invited to share with adults in faith traditions, these experiences impact them, and they sense that they are important to adults. Adults provide role models as children observe adults taking seriously the rituals of their faith communities.

Josiah challenges us to take seriously the Word of God. His voice inspires us to show respect for the Word of God just as he challenged his own people to do the same. Children must be taught to honor God's Word. Responsibility for study of God's Word falls upon adults and children alike. Study of God's Word is a lifelong endeavor. We help our children grow in their faith when we take time to tell them Bible stories. Giving children their own Bibles appropriate for their age level inspires them to continue to read God's Word as they grow older. Josiah believed that individuals were never too old to study the Bible and learn from its teachings. We do well to follow in his footsteps and heed his instructions.

Some of us erect false idols in our lives. Often, we allow these idols to control our lives, and we worship them rather than God. Naming our idols often gives us the resolve to destroy them and put God first in our lives. The culture around us presents us with many tempting enticements that we sometimes find hard to resist. Josiah offers us another alternative. He instructs and commands us to remove any false idols from our lives and turn to God for guidance, strength, and direction.

Many of us are blessed with influential leaders like Josiah. Listening to these leaders helps us make necessary changes in our lives for the better. Apparently Josiah was very persuasive and charismatic in his approach toward leadership. His people trusted him to lead, and they followed his instructions. When such competent leaders appear in our lives, we do well to listen to their advice and follow their admonitions. God gives us such leaders for a purpose. God desires us to follow in the right path, and inspirational leaders often take us there if we are willing to be led. When we humble ourselves to these leaders, we find that we are obedient to God's will for our lives. Honoring and respecting the spiritual leaders God brings into our lives helps us to develop into people that please God.

The Bible informs us that Josiah remained true to God throughout his reign. He kept faithful to God's teachings and did not desert them. He remained true to his calling as a child king and used the instructions and guidance of his youth to carry him forward as he served the people as an adult. This rigorous devotion to God's laws positively impacted the entire kingdom of Judah. Often, individuals start out in life trying to follow God's ways, but they get side-stepped by temptations that deter them. Josiah apparently conquered his desire for these enticements. He managed to resist them and forged ahead with a clear conscience and steady voice. Children today desire guidance from adults as they move from childhood to adulthood. They emulate individuals who steer them in the right direction and insist they remain true to their faith in God even when life is challenging. Children need to follow in the footsteps of adults who remain steady in their faith, do not constantly change back and forth, and seek to build their faith on a solid foundation. Adults who claim to believe one set of teachings but demonstrate the exact opposite are not positive role models for children. We confuse children when we tell them we value God and God's teachings, but fail to demonstrate our beliefs or neglect our faith.

Josiah's voice matured as he grew older. His voice changed from that of a child king to that of an adult sovereign. His voice spoke with authority as he emerged from childhood into adulthood. Josiah found himself equipped to speak with such a powerful voice, no doubt because of the adults who helped him find his voice and articulate his mission. Forces at work in his life played a pivotal role in his childhood so that he eventually spoke with passion. The scriptures do not list for us the role models, encouragers, and teachers that Josiah surely encountered in his life as he grew from boyhood to manhood. Yet somewhere in his reign he dedicated himself to the highest ideals of servanthood. He encountered people who guided him, and he sought out opportunities to grow in his faith. He developed into a trusted king. Children today also seek after positive role models: teachers, pastors, friends, and mentors who point them in the right direction and provide them with positive examples of mature living. These faith partners work alongside children as they listen, discipline, encourage, and demonstrate for them good choices and wise decision-making.

One believes, however, that Josiah often pushed himself to learn, apart from the mentoring of others. He possessed a strong faith and a desire to seek after knowledge. He also showed a humble spirit and contrite heart. When the high priest discovered the Law of the Lord in the temple, this remarkable discovery convinced Josiah of the past sins of his people and their need for repentance. He took immediate and swift action to correct the past and bring his people into a close relationship with God. When adults observe children today who possess the same compassionate, humble spirit as Josiah, they must affirm these children. These adults also learn a lesson from observing these children as they submit their lives to God. Many adults find themselves brought closer to God as they observe children pledging allegiance to God's ways. We adults do well to emulate these children.

The voice of Josiah continues to impact us today as we read his story and listen to his admonitions to his people to return to God. Like Josiah, we have choices to make. Will we continue to live with past mistakes, thinking they bind us forever? Or rather will we turn to the future God has planned for us? Will we be loyal to the worthy, steadfast, and honored religious traditions we have learned, or will we neglect these traditions as trivial and not worth our time? Will we teach our children these traditions, or will we ignore them so they cease to impact and influence future generations of believers? Like Josiah, will we turn to God's Word, revere God's Word, read God's Word, teach its lessons to our children, and let its rich truths permeate our lives? As a child king, Josiah makes choices that ultimately determine the direction of his nation and his own life. Today, we have choices to make that ultimately determine the outcome of our communities, churches, schools, and our own individual lives. Like Josiah, we must choose wisely and let our voices sound out with shouts of praise and honor to God.

QUESTIONS FOR REFLECTION AND DISCUSSION

1. How can people "walk in the way of the Lord" today? What intentional steps can they take in their faith development?

2. Reflect on the ways you study God's Word. Are you a diligent student?

3. How do we teach children today to respect God's Word? How do we teach biblical truths to a new generation of believers?

4. What are the traditions in your family and church that are meaningful to you?

5. Discuss some of the ways your church is teaching children the traditions of your faith. What are the rituals that the children in your congregation find meaningful?

6. Reflect on people you know who have demonstrated courage and broken the unhealthy chains of their past to live new, changed lives.

7. What does the word *repentance* mean to you? What does your church teach about repentance, and how do you practice this concept in your own life?

8. Discuss ways you see God working in the lives of the children in your congregation.

9. Share about the importance of Bible stories for children. Reflect on ways your congregation teaches Bible stories to children.

10. Think about children you know who demonstrate a teachable spirit. Name these children, and offer prayers of thanksgiving.

PART TWO:
Stories From The New Testament

Children Cry Out In Praise

Read the Story: Matthew 21: 12–16

> *Jesus said to them, "Out of the mouths of*
> *infants and nursing babies you have prepared*
> *praise for yourself?"*

Matthew 21: 16b (NRSV)

One-year-old Will Turner, along with his parents, attend Connell Memorial United Methodist in Goodlettsville, Tennessee. During a recent worship service Will began to utter "baby talk." He was especially vocal during the sermon time. Both pastors of the congregation view the cooing and chattering of infants as a joy rather than a distraction. They did not consider Will's speech to be a bother or disruption. Yet, like most first-time parents, his mom, Kelly, and father, Billy, thought Will might be a little too loud with his presence in the sanctuary on that particular morning.

After the completion of the worship service, the associate pastor made her way to the back of the sanctuary and greeted the worshippers. When Will's family approached, she shook hands with his parents and gave him a hug. Will's mother apologized for Will's constant babbling during the service, but the associate pastor assured her that there was absolutely nothing wrong with Will crying out his words of praise in the midst of the sanctuary. She reminded the Turners of Jesus' words in the gospel of Matthew, which read, "Out of the mouths of infants and babes, you have ordained praise." The mother jokingly commented that she was not sure how much praise has issued forth from her child's lips! The pastor and family laughed together.

Then, the pastor informed the family that children worship God in their own distinct ways, ways that are often very different from that of adults in the faith community. God endows even babies and infants with the gift of praise, she told them. After her comments, the Turner family left worship knowing that Will was loved and affirmed rather than viewed as a disruptive child who needed to be silenced.

How wonderful it would have been if the religious leaders in the temple, during the time of Jesus, had viewed children in the same way. Rather, they harshly vocalized their concerns to Jesus that the praising children were a distraction, and they needed to be silenced. Not only that, but they were actually angry with the children. Very little time passed before they loudly and belligerently voiced their complaints to Jesus.

The gospel writer Matthew understands the passionate praise offered by children in the temple, and he lifts up the voices of children rather than stifling them. His text amazingly centers on the praise of children rather than the praise of adults. His affirmation takes place in a setting—the temple,—which is most often pictured in the gospels as an adult place of worship. Yet here were children shouting out their praise to Jesus with loud, jubilant voices.

Have you ever heard even one sermon preached on the voices of these children crying out in the temple? Have you read even one devotional reading or listened to even one talk reminding us of the power of the praises of these children? If you have, you are in a unique position. We often scurry over the words and actions of these children. We fail to hear their fervent cries. We ignore their honorable praise. We shut our ears to their uplifting adorations. We close our eyes to their risk-taking attempts at worship. We tune out our hearts to their childlike faith. We forget that Jesus heartily commended them for their worship and spoke forceful words back to the religious leaders. Jesus believed that the children's words and actions were important and worthwhile, and so should we.

Biblical readers often place significance on Matthew 21 since it is packed with several important events in the life of Jesus. We easily ignore the section that highlights the children. We make the mistake of centering on what we perceive as more important stories.

After all, prior to the story of the children praising, we read that Jesus entered Jerusalem riding on a donkey. The Palm Sunday story is important to our Christian tradition and certainly a worthy story to focus our attention upon. Then immediately following the Palm Sunday incident, we read the story of Jesus cleansing the temple, a story that reminds us of the necessity of prayer and dignity in our worship settings. Also, Matthew tells us that Jesus entered the temple and healed the blind and lame. Jesus' miracles always intrigue us, so we naturally gravitate to those biblical stories, do we not?

Is there any room in the gospel's crowded text for Christian readers to even begin to lift out, focus on, and find meaning in the story of the children? Too often, their story remains buried in the text, hidden away by adults who read the other stories surrounding this one, but somehow never let the story of the children praising Jesus have center stage. When we take this approach, we do injustice to the story, to the biblical children, and to the efforts of our own children today as they seek to worship Jesus.

It is time for the voices of the children in the temple to be loudly and clearly heard! So, let us hear their voices. Let us carefully listen and humbly hear their poignant words. Let us promise not to hurry along or partially listen. No, we must give these children our undivided attention. For they teach us lessons on how to relate to children today when they too lift their voices in praise.

However, looking at their story in the context of the surrounding stories in Matthew's text helps us to better appreciate and more fully comprehend the story of the children. So, we take a few moments to review the setting for our story and the prior actions that influence the children and cause them to be present in the temple on that particular day.

Chapter 21 of Matthew's gospel begins with Jesus entering Jerusalem, riding on a lowly donkey as a symbol of his own humility. The politically charged crowds shout, "Hosanna," which translates from the Hebrew as "please save us" or "save now." Theirs was a cry for freedom and deliverance from the hated Roman government. Their words also constituted praise. No doubt the children now praising in the temple were present with their parents when Jesus entered Jerusalem. On that day, which we in Christian tradition call Palm Sunday, we imagine the children as they mingled among the crowds. We envision that they, like their parents and adult friends, waved palm branches and heralded Jesus as their deliverer from oppression.

Influenced and impacted by the Palm Sunday incident, these children later moved to the temple area, where they continued their praises long after the cries of the adults ceased. We might wonder where the parents of these children were. These parents' lives could be in danger if they shouted their praises in the heavily guarded temple during Passover. The Roman authorities observed the waving of palm branches, knowing full well that these leaves represented the national symbol of independence for the Jewish nation. They also were aware that Jesus was very popular with the common people, so popular that he had become their hope for deliverance. The frenzied actions of the crowd tipped off the authorities. They reasoned that the adult palm wavers needed to be closely watched, especially for any signs of rebellion and possible rioting. Yet who would pay attention to a few children slipping into the temple area to worship?

It is only later that the religious authorities recognized the impact of the children's words. These children demonstrated worship on behalf of all those whose voices were stifled. In a sense, these children offered praise on behalf of all the Jewish people who feared for their very lives, yet carried the seed of hope that they placed upon the shoulders of a humble donkey-riding Messiah.

The children who praised Jesus exhibited joyful passionate, and unfettered praise. Neither meek nor passive in their worship, their exuberant shouts drew the angry attention of the temple authorities, and these unnerved adults hoped to quickly silence the children's voices. However, they could not be silenced. They were praising Jesus in the way children often worship: with loud voices, with dancing and swaying, and with jubilant motion.

Unlike the adults who found the worship of these children disruptive and unsettling, Jesus honored the praise of the children and refused to silence them. Instead, Jesus silenced the voices of the adults. He informed the children's critics that their praise was ordained in scripture. Going back to the words of the psalmist found in Psalm 8:2, Jesus reminded the adults that the worship of children pleases God. Furthermore, Jesus taught that God gifts young children, even infants, with the capacity to worship.

In our opening story, Will's parents and his faith community recognized, like Jesus did, that children possess the God-given ability to worship. Yet children worship in their own unique ways that are very different from adults. Will's pastor refused to let Will's parents think for one moment that their son was disruptive in worship. Just because children do not worship in the same ways as adults does not render their worship any less valuable. God hears the voices of children when they worship. God knows their innocent hearts. God listens to their cries. God watches their motions. And God is pleased.

Adults must acknowledge that children can worship and desire to. They must also understand that children praise God in their own unique ways. These are two important concepts that change the way many adults view children in the worshiping community. When adults realize that children can indeed worship, but may do so in their own childlike ways, these faith friends gain more patience and respect for children. Children are then welcomed into the sanctuary, mentored in by family and church members, and taught how to praise. Congregants grant children the freedom to act as children in worship, and they are patient as they learn how to offer praise and thanksgiving in ways that honor God. Rather than view the worship of children as disruptive, they understand that children worship as children, not as adults. Rather than criticize and scold children, they recognize that children naturally squirm and wiggle in the pew. They may loudly whisper honest questions to parents. They might draw a picture of the pastor. They often yawn during prayer. They sometimes giddily wave their hands along with the music director. They can freely lift their hands in praise or sway to the music.

Children learn best in worship when they engage their senses. They taste the Communion bread, they reach out and touch the pastor's stole, they smell the altar flowers, they hear the choir anthems, and they stare at the stained-glass windows. And like the children in the temple, their loud voices and active motions can often be heard above the subdued voices and restrained action of adult worshippers.

Like the authorities in the temple, we too often try to silence the voices of children in worship. We give children the unattainable command to sit still and the unrealistic challenge to keep silent. In doing so, we imply that children's voices have no place in worship. Yet Jesus demands that the voices of children be heard, respected, and honored. Jesus made his viewpoint loud and clear during his last journey to the temple in Jerusalem. When he visits our sanctuaries today, he comes with the same appeal: let the children be heard.

Are we willing to hear the voices of our children as they praise Jesus? We must! For God orders, authorizes, decrees, confirms, and honors the voices of children. So, let the voices of children burst forth with hosannas, with fervent praise that is acceptable and pleasing to God. Let adults keep silent and listen.

Questions For Reflection And Discussion

1. How does your congregation treat children in the worship setting?

2. Name some ways you observe children worshiping. How do these ways differ from adult worship? How are they alike?

3. When children have a role in worship, such as singing in the children's choir, do you see them in the role of worship leaders or performers?

4. How do you and your congregation react to crying babies or disruptive children in the worship setting?

5. What are some ways congregations can help parents during worship? What role do you have as a faith friend to children?

6. In what ways can churches teach children how to worship in ways that are helpful?

7. Name some ways your congregation allows children to serve in the worship setting Do you see positive or negative results when children have leadership roles?

8. What are some additional ways your congregation can involve children in worship?

9. Discuss the advantages and disadvantages of having children in the sanctuary during worship. Discuss the pros and cons of children's church.

10. Discuss ways in which congregations can help children use their senses in the worship setting. Name some ways you think children use their senses in worship.

A Child Shares His Lunch

Read the Story: John 6:1–14

> *There is a boy here who has five barley loaves*
> *and two fish. But what are they among so*
> *many people?*

John 6:9 (NRSV)

When Blaze Trumble of Boulder City, Las Vegas turned six years old, he made the decisions to collect for the homeless in his community. He was able to gather 254 full-size blankets, 10 baby blankets, and $1,340 in donations. He then distributed the blankets to the homeless at the Las Vegas Rescue Mission on the afternoon and evening before Thanksgiving. When reporters asked how he came up with the idea for this humanitarian gesture, the kindergarten student remarked, "I just kind of thought of it. People just don't have anything, and they need something to keep them warm." His vision for this project actually started when Blaze reached the age of five years old. At that time, he surprised his father when he told him that rather than receiving present for his birthday, he wanted permission to collect blankets for the homeless. Permission granted![16]

With winter getting colder, seven-year-old Logan Snyder of Laguna Niguel, California, worried about the homeless. He expressed his concern to his mother one evening. His friend, eight-year- old Marcos Santos, overheard their conversation and joined in with his opinion. Marcos suggested that perhaps he and Logan could collect blankets and jackets. So the boys got busy writing fliers and passing them out in their community. Two days later, they collected more than a truck bed's worth of clothing articles, much more than they had hoped for. Before donating the items to a local mission, the boys sorted and washed the clothes. They envision a future food drive and shoe drive.[17]

About two thousand years ago, a young boy, whose age we do not know, sat placidly on a hillside, lunch box in tow, and listened quietly to Jesus as he taught the crowd. Soon the hungry students grumbled and complained about their lack of food. Disciple Andrew searched the horde of people, looking for any available resources. Eventually he noticed the lunch of the young boy, but discovered this lad only had five loaves and two fish. He doubtingly remarked to Jesus that this boy's meager offering surely would not be enough to feed the large crowds. Jesus thought otherwise and proved it when he used the boy's lunch to feed five thousand men, in addition to many women and children! Yet like Blaze, Logan, and Marcos, this boy had to be willing to sacrifice in order for Jesus' miracle to take place.

Can it be that there were others in the crowd that day, besides this young boy, who also brought their own food supply? Perhaps these people either hid their food or refused to give up their treats when Andrew approached. John's gospel leads us to believe that the lad readily gave his lunch to Andrew. We cannot imagine Andrew snatching the boy's lunch away without the child's permission. Perhaps others failed to share because they were greedy, selfish, or just plain hungry. The text leaves out details that we wish we knew. Our minds work to fill in missing pieces of the story, even if we admit that the gospel writer provides us little detail.

We like to think that the boy's mother lovingly fixed his lunch that morning, knowing full well that her son would definitely become hungry as the day wore on. If this child acted anything like the active and growing children we know, we can be certain that he would soon becomes really hungry and look forward to the delicious meal in his basket. Also, we form a picture in our minds of this boy thinking that his mother might be upset with him for giving away his carefully prepared lunch. We simply do not know if the details we envision are correct. The text remains absent. One thing emerges for sure.

Somewhere along the way, this child pushed aside his hunger pangs, he dismissed his selfish desires, he forgot his childish worries, and he offered his lunch to Jesus. He remembered his childhood teaching, instilled in him from the time he was born, that his heritage called him to practice hospitality.

Did the adults present with Jesus forget their religious mandate to extend hospitality at all times and in all places? Did they neglect their Jewish teaching that marked them as a distinct nation bound together by generosity for the needy? Did they ignore their duty to share with others? Did they let their hunger pains rule over their command to show compassion? Did this young boy's example stir others to remove their food from carefully concealed hiding places? Convicted of their failure as God's people, did they then remember their heritage and repentantly begin to selflessly share with others around them? While we ponder these puzzling questions, for which our gospel writer John provides us no precise answers, at least we can certainly be clear about one thing. This boy's actions became pivotal to the outcome of our story. Without his willingness to share, the amazing miracle that captivates our attention could not have taken place on the hillside on that day. Without the boy's help, Jesus was left with no food to bless.

A child partnered with Jesus, and a miracle took place! Reminding ourselves of the pivotal role of a child in this poignant story in no way diminishes the miraculous event or Jesus' powerful part in the narrative. After all, even when extremely hungry people ate their fill, Jesus offered more. Twelve baskets of food provided leftovers for the disciples, who busied themselves waiting on the crowd of hungry takers. Jesus blessed, people ate, and disciples served. Jesus multiplied, hunger ceased, and mercy abounded. Only Jesus fed the famished the way they needed to be fed: with overflowing baskets of abundant grace. Yet grace began with a child's simple gift of five loaves and two fish.

In the modern stories at the beginning of this chapter, we discover three children who partnered with Jesus to make a difference for the homeless in their own communities. In these places, like the biblical hillside setting, miracles happen as well. Children reach out, children sacrifice, and children give warm gifts to shelter the homeless from the cold. Their caring, unselfish actions are reminiscent of the sacrifice of the lad in our Bible story. Blaze, Logan, and Marcos provided blankets. An unnamed lad in the Bible offered his lunch. The modern-day children are separated from the boy in John's gospel by different times, divergent settings, and dissimilar circumstances, but not by their clarity of purpose: all the children committed themselves to give in order to benefit others.

A child's practice of radical hospitality in the biblical story causes us to take notice of his sharing, which ultimately results in a surprising and miraculous outcome. It is time to grant this unnamed child the credit due him. We honestly admit that we find his action worthy of commendation and his example of Christlike service worthy of imitation. A child deserves our praise and thanks. A child teaches adults what it means to willingly give and share. Have we given this child our full attention? He wants us to follow his example. He wants us to offer our gifts to God. He wants us to partner with God so that miracles may happen. Are we willing to follow his example? Or, like the greedy crowds, do we hide our gifts and refuse to give them up?

Adults often mimic the attitude of Andrew in the biblical story when dealing with children in the present. They know that children have gifts to offer, but they believe that those gifts are too small, too insignificant. Andrew thought that the boy's lunch was insufficient for feeding the crowd. We sometimes mistakenly impose this same way of thinking when children wish to serve. We tell ourselves that children are too young and their gifts are too little to make a difference. How wrong we are!

The stories of children collecting blankets for the homeless are but two of a multitude of stories about children reaching out to others with godly love. Get on the Internet, and you will discover story after story of children putting their faith into practice in unselfish ways. Many of these children sacrifice enormous amounts of their time and resources to alleviate suffering and practice compassion. We all know children who continually engage in mission and service. Adults must offer their support, their praise, and their affirmation to these children. The text does not tell us, but surely the one who blessed little children blessed the lad in John's gospel. Hopefully, his mother, family members, and community affirmed and praised him as well when he returned home and shared his story. God's love compels us to do the same for our children.

Adults must also partner with children. Children deserve lessons in ways to give. They merit our patience, our attention, and our time. Working with children in mission requires diligence and fortitude. Often, adults find it easier to do the mission work by themselves or work with other adults and youth, but determine to leave children completely out of the picture. This kind of unhealthy attitude hinders children in their efforts to be good stewards. Children yearn for mature stewardship mentors who guide and direct their childlike efforts. Children seek adults who affirm them. When we confront caring children, but shun their efforts and show our prejudice toward their stewardship efforts, we discourage these children. Time and again children prove adults wrong. Children surprise us with their gifts and abilities. When we keep an honest, open, yet realistic opinion of children and their gifts, they amaze us with all they can do and all they have to offer.

Never believe for one moment that the gifts of children are insignificant. God views the gifts of our children as precious and honorable, and so should adults. Jesus made it clear to Andrew that the lunch of the unnamed boy was in no way insignificant; rather, he used it to feed a multitude of people. God takes the gifts of children, multiplies them, and uses them to feed the world. God uses all of our gifts in the same loving manner. God takes our gifts, blesses them, and multiplies them, no matter how small or insignificant they may seem to us. Now, that constitutes a miracle!

Like the gracious act of hospitality expressed by the child in John's gospel, the radical acts of hospitality shared by children today often go unnoticed. Yet adults who make children a priority, like Jesus did, will not only praise and affirm children for their efforts, but also will continually teach children how to carry out deeds that are radical and life-changing.

Over two thousand years ago, a young boy brought his lunch to Jesus. Jesus greatly needed that lunch, and the boy generously gave it. In reality, his lunch was really the *one* and *only* thing Jesus needed that day, along with the boy's loyalty and trust. The lad gave all of these things to Jesus. Consider this truth. A child held in his hands the *one* and *only* thing Jesus needed to bring a miracle to fruition. Often, the one and only thing Jesus needs from us are the very things we keep securely locked in our possession, refusing to surrender.

Will we greedily and tightly hold on to our lunch boxes with clenched and closed fists or, like the boy, will we readily give Jesus our lunches so others can be fed? When we let go, we set our gifts free so that Jesus can miraculously use them, bless them, and increase them. No gifts lovingly given from the beloved children of God prove to be insignificant. Just ask a boy with five loaves and two fish.

QUESTIONS FOR REFLECTION AND DISCUSSION

1. John does not tell us if any of the boy's family was present at the feeding of the five thousand. Imagine the boy returning home to share the details of his encounter with Jesus. What do you think he shared, and how do you think his family reacted?

2. Do you think the lad taught the crowd any lessons on hospitality, or do you think the people were too caught up in their hunger to pay attention to the example of a young boy sharing his lunch?

3. What are some ways children share with you?

4. In what ways have you viewed the gifts of children as insignificant? In what ways have you viewed them as significant?

5. Discuss some ways you have seen children putting radical hospitality into practice.

6. What gifts have you been given by God that you can use to share with others?

7. What ways are your congregation allowing children to use their gifts in service?

8. How have you and your congregation affirmed and blessed the gifts of children?

9. Name some ways families can work together to extend radical hospitality to those in need.

10. Honestly share ways you have failed to surrender your gifts to Jesus.

Endnotes

16. Fred Couzens, "Boy Collects Blankets for Homeless at Rescue Mission," *Downtown View* (http://www.viewnews.com/2008/VIEW-Dec-09-/Tue-2008/downtown/25523806.htmnl).

17. Joseph Espiritu, "Laguna Niguel Boys Collect Blankets, Jackets for the Homeless," *OC Register.com* (http://articles.ocregister.com/2010-12-20/news/25294129_1_blankets-jackets-collection-drive).

Children Refuse To Play

Read the Story: Luke 7:31–35

> *To what then will I compare the people of this*
> *generation, and what are they like? They are*
> *like children sitting in the marketplace and*
> *calling to one another, "We played the flute*
> *for you, and you did not dance; we wailed*
> *and you did not weep."*

Luke 7:31–32 (NRSV)

Nine-year-old Rita Barlow lives in a neighborhood filled with children. When she enthusiastically runs outside to play, Brian, a neighborhood boy, appears, bringing his new ball to show to Rita. Rita notices other neighborhood children soon appear, so she suggests they use the new ball to play a game of kickball, her favorite sport. Brian agrees, and Rita begins dividing the children into two teams. Soon the game is underway. However, each time that Brian kicks the ball and runs toward first base, he ends up being tagged out by a skilled player on the opposing team. Brian incessantly whines and complains. He claims he is not out, even though it is obvious to the other children that his opponents defeat him fairly. However, in order to keep peace, the children allow Brian's team an extra out. Yet nothing seems to appease Brian. Finally, he refuses to play and ends up grabbing his kickball away from the other children, leaving the game, and madly stomping off toward his house.

Brian reminds us of the children in the marketplace in Luke's gospel. The children whined and complained about the game they were playing. Nothing seemed to satisfy the petulant children who refused to play any game the other children suggested. Like Brian, they were spoiled sports. Yet they appeared to be even more disagreeable than Brian. Their tirade escalated to the point that the game never even commenced, and the playground fun ceased before the game began. The text allows the reader to hear their bickering voices as they called to one another in the marketplace.

Jesus watched children noisily playing in the Palestinian village marketplace, a common sight in his time and one he observed repeatedly. He used their inhospitality toward one another as an example of the hostility for his own ministry and that of John the Baptist. In particular, Jesus focused upon the shallow attitudes of the scribes and Pharisees who always blinded themselves to truth, criticized both his and John's teachings, and found fault with their diametrically opposed lifestyles.

The marketplace game turned out to be a common team game of that era played by Jewish children that perhaps Jesus viewed as he spoke his words of warning. The game consisted of two teams of children. One team played the flute while the other team danced like participants at a wedding. Then the action of the game changed. When one team wailed, the other team grieved, like mourners at a funeral. At least that was the way the game was supposed to be played. Sometimes playing children cooperated and the game moved along without any problems. However, Jesus noticed that other times, children initially gather to play the game, but ended up refusing to cooperate with one another and acted sullen. These moody children decided not to participate in the action, even though in the beginning they agreed to play the game according to the set rules.

Jesus compared the actions of the playing children in the marketplace to the attitude of the scribes and Pharisees toward his and John the Baptist's ministry. Even though God called both Jesus and John to Baptist to proclaim the reign and power of God's kingdom, John and Jesus brought contrasting lifestyles and differing messages. Yet their critics found fault with both of them. They neglected to understand that God could bring redemption through various means and messengers.

Jesus' ministry compared to the part of the games in which the children played the flute and danced. His ministry proved to be a time of rejoicing and joy. Jesus ate and partied with tax collectors, prostitutes, and sinners. He welcomed the downcast. He lifted up the suffering. He celebrated life to the fullest. His critics called him a glutton and drunkard. They disapprovingly recognized him as a friend of tax collectors and sinners.

In contrast, John the Baptist's ministry turned out to be somber. John ate no bread and drank no wine. John neither attended parties nor ate lavish meals. John dressed eccentrically and ate locust. John refused to celebrate life; rather, he humbly baptized repentant sinners in the Jordan River. His critics believed a demon possessed John the Baptist.

With stubborn unbelief and spiritual blindness, those who criticized Jesus and John the Baptist wished them to reverse their actions, just like the children in the game switched roles as the game played out. They wanted Jesus to act like wailing children playing a funeral game and wanted John the Baptist to dance to the piper as if at a wedding. Since they refused to reverse their roles, the complainers rejected both, just as the dour, unhappy children decided not to play either game. Even if Jesus and John agreed to reserve their roles, this would not silence their accusers, for they acted like sulking children.

Apparently the scribes and Pharisees were not the only ones who opposed the divergent ministries of Jesus and John the Baptist. Jesus spoke of a childish generation of unbelievers who fervently disapproved of these two ministries. Nothing God did pleased these doubters. God sent Jesus and John to proclaim truth to the present generation. Yet this generation denied and evaded the truth. They sought to destroy the reputation of Jesus and John. They refused to mourn to John's lament or dance to Jesus' happy tune. Since neither John nor Jesus lived up to their unreasonable expectations, they criticized and condemned both men and their ministries. We can soften the voices of the children by reasoning that they, at least, are children, often prone to quarreling among themselves. We rationalize the children's actions as childish, but not unreasonable for children who have not matured into adults. However, we find it difficult to justify the petty actions of childish, critical adults.

Luke concludes his story by saying, "Wisdom is indicated by all her children" (Luke 7: 35). Luke teaches us that wisdom proves itself by the behavior it produces. Those who faulted Jesus and John the Baptist for their ministries proved to be unwise. Their actions validated them as such. Jesus compared the present generation with the children in the marketplace whose prejudice marked them as judgmental, intolerant, and spiritually blind. These individuals closed their eyes to the work of God in their present time and place. As a result of their spiritual blindness, these people missed out on the kingdom of God that unexpectedly sprung forth in both vibrant ministries of Jesus and John the Baptist. God validated and blessed two diverse ministries and two unique messengers, but some in that present generation lacked the wisdom to discern this truth. Do we lack this wisdom also?

Even though the voices of children in the marketplace offer us sounds that are neither appealing nor affirming, nevertheless, these children's voices are important and teach us valuable lessons of God's judgment and grace. Even if they are not the pleasant voices we wish to hear from children, we must listen. Their harsh tones and mocking jeers remind us of our own voices at times as we consider our relationship with God. We often speak to God in unfriendly tones with belligerent voices. Sometimes, like Brian in our opening story, we wish to take our ball home rather than play by the rules God sets for us.

Furthermore, Jesus' teachings about the voices of these neighborhood children reveal for us important truths about God's relationship with us. John the Baptist focused on God's judgment, while Jesus emphasized God's grace. We need to hear and reflect on both elements of their teachings in order to understand God, God's work in our world today, and God's action in the past and in the future. Sometimes God judges us for failing to live up to God's commandments and purposes. Other times, God judges us by what we do with the privileges and opportunities God gives us. God asks us to repent of our failings and grants us the strength to begin again. God tempers judgment with abundant grace and offers mercy, love, and compassion to each of us even in our times of failure and sin. Each day holds the opportunity for renewed commitments to God's ways and purposes. While we accept God's judgments, we yearn for God's forgiveness and grace.

Churchgoers sometimes easily find fault with the ministry of today's messengers of God and categorize their ministries as ineffective, much as the doubters did in the time of Jesus. John the Baptist and Jesus remind us that God uses different preachers with distinct methods. One teaching we glean from the biblical story is that God sends many different types of messengers today just as God did in biblical times. God endows each with the gifts and skills he or she needs to proclaim God's Word and to bring about God's kingdom. God uses a variety of individuals and myriad gifts.

Jesus speaks to us through the gospel writer Luke and suggests that we honor, respect, and support the messengers that God sends our way. This important suggestion in no way erases our need to hold our religious leaders accountable to the highest standards of conduct and integrity. Yet we validate the uniqueness of each pastor's ministry when we recognize individual gifts and graces. We exhibit maturity when we refuse to constantly criticize our God-appointed leaders or show favoritism for one leader over another. God empowers each leader with unique gifts for ministry. We harm and weaken the ministries of our pastors and demonstrate immature childishness when we model ourselves after the children in the marketplace.

Committed leaders learn quickly that some people cannot be pleased, no matter what the leader does or says. The closed mind finds fault with others. The closed heart finds excuses not to respond to the gospel, no matter how effectively the messenger presents the good news. Some individuals get caught up with their own belief systems. Thus, they refuse to even consider another opinion or new ideas that might help them grow and enlarge their faith. Sadly, they reject the idea that if they would just stop, listen, and consider new ideas or differing opinions, they might be changed for the better. These individuals have difficulty looking at issues from another perspective. Instead, they belittle the messenger who brings a message different from their own. Like Jesus and John the Baptist, leaders today must serve with the assurance of their own calling and be confident of their own gifts for ministry. Otherwise, immature childish people can shatter the pastor's confidence in his or her calling.

What do the children's games have to do with the kingdom of God? What do the children's voices have to tell us today? The children in Luke's gospel reacted with disappointment when their playmates refused to play their game. Their voices calling in the marketplace lacked the ability to induce the other children to join in their musical medley. We believers understand that the message of the kingdom of God proclaims both good news and great joy to the listener, but provides a warning for those who refuse to hear. Some do not know this; others reject this reality. Today, the enticements of the world often overshadow the voices of truth in our own world. Like the generation of Jesus' time, our age marks itself with indifference and contempt, especially in regards to spiritual matters. Indifference dulls our ears to hear God's voice and dims our hearts to the good news of the gospel.

The image of scornful children who refuse to participate may well describe Jesus' generation and our own. Many people today are uncommitted to Christ or the church. They watch from the sidelines of life and heap ridicule on the committed Christian faith. If a preacher speaks of the concept of sin, these people label him or her as too conservative, not positive enough, and out of touch with modern life. If a preacher speaks of grace for the sinner, these individuals label him or her as too liberal, too social-minded, and not spiritual enough. Can we hear Jesus' voice today? Do we know our own voices to be like those of the ill-tempered children in the marketplace? Will we remain petulant children unwilling to change?

In Luke's gospel, God offered those who originally heard the words two very different approaches to the way God sought to redeem the world. One came through Jesus, and the other came through John the Baptist. The people wind up rejecting both! The very best God offered was not good enough for those sulking and scornful children. How do we handle the way God tries to save us today? It is easy to point an accusing finger at the people of Jesus' time. However, we face the chronic condition of dissatisfaction also. Jesus came into the world to save us from this condition of discontent. Jesus comes to offers us new life, abundant life. God gifts us with the ability to see all things new, which is the beginning of grateful and joyful living.

Are we more like the scornful, sulking children who refused to play a game in the marketplace? Do we refuse to open our eyes, ears, hearts, and minds to the possibility of God's truth being offered to use in a variety of new and exciting ways? Are we like petulant children, so ill-tempered and set in our ways that we shut out any messenger who does not meet our criteria? Are we like the child Brian who did not get his way so he took his ball home and refused to play? When we do not get our way, do we selfishly take our ball home and keep others from playing and participating in the joy of the game of life?

Or will we instead act in the exact opposite way of Brian and the children in the marketplace? Will we embrace life in all of its creative goodness? Will we joyfully dance to the music, mournfully sing our dirges, and gladly abandon ourselves to the game of life, remembering that Jesus Christ himself comes and plays with his children?

So, how should we play this game? When Jesus comes to play, he arrives singing the dirge song of his own death, and we mourn. He arrives playing the flute tune of own resurrection and we dance. Together, we play the game of resurrection and new life. In this game, there are no losers. Every one of God's children wins, every time. Only one rule applies. Those children who wish to participate actually have to play the game, not sit on the sidelines and complain.

QUESTIONS FOR REFLECTION AND DISCUSSION

1. How do you view the ministry of John the Baptist? How were the ministry of Jesus and John the Baptist different?

2. How did God use both the ministries of John the Baptist and Jesus to proclaim the kingdom of God?

3. Think about the ministers you know in your own congregation or in past congregations in which you have worshiped. How were these ministers treated by the congregation and by you?

4. Reflect on whether you have an open mind to new ideas or a closed mind. How can you open your mind to embrace new ideas?

5. How do you address critics of the church and pastors in general?

6. How do you show appreciation to your own pastor?

7. What is the difference between wisdom and knowledge? How does Jesus speak of wisdom in our Bible story?

8. Reflect on ways you refuse to play by God's rules and instead set your own rules. How does this harm you in your walk with God?

9. Discuss the ways God uses both elements of judgment and grace in our lives.

10. How do you extend love to critical people in your congregation, yet challenge them to change their attitudes?

A Child Asks Questions

Read the Story: Luke 2:41–52

> *After three days, they found him in the*
> *Temple, sitting among the teachers, listening*
> *to them and asking them questions. And*
> *all who heard him were amazed at his*
> *understanding and his answers.*
>
> Luke 2:46–47 (NRSV)

Reverend Paul Gardner works diligently with the confirmation class at Connell Memorial United Methodist. Five six-grade students enlist in the preparatory membership class and ready themselves for church membership. Today, they sit in a circle on the floor and dialogue with Rev. Gardner, who is known with affection as Pastor Paul. Pastor Paul allows the students to fire off question after question about religious matters, and he attempts, to the best of his ability, to answer these questions honestly. He also invites the students to express their own opinions and admonishes members of the confirmation class to listen carefully when others speak and to respect the ideas others share. Pastor Paul converses with the students in such an open and courteous manner that they come away excited about their learning experience. They also recognize Pastor Paul as a wise teacher of the law.

No other gospel writer records the story of Jesus, at the age of twelve, as he listened and questioned the teachers of the Law. Luke informs us that Jesus sat in the temple area, both listening and questioning the rabbis of his day. Luke fails to inform us exactly what questions Jesus asked, but one imagines the conversation between Jesus and the teachers involved theological questions, questions about God and about the laws of Judaism.

Following this pivotal event in the life of Jesus, we find his parents frantically searching for their twelve-year-old son. Readers often center on this part of the story, a section where Jesus seemed to disobey his parents, upset them, excuse his action, and embarrass his mother. This section of the story often overshadows the voice of Jesus as he asked questions, received answers, and expressed his own thoughts on theological matters. Luke makes it quite clear that Jesus amazed those present with his understanding and his answers. Yet we sometimes push aside the voice of a twelve-year-old boy, even if that boy is Jesus, in favor of time spent wrestling with the story of Jesus getting lost and eventually being found. So before we can even hear the voice of Jesus, we must address his separation from his parents.

Parents easily relate to the story as it sounds to them like a typical twelve-year-old. When we examine the story, it helps for us to picture both the humanity of Jesus and the divinity of Christ. As we read scripture, frequently we struggle to know when one emerges and the other comes into play. Luke does not intend for us to solve this tension; rather, he wants us to comprehend that the boy Jesus obviously struggled with his own destiny and call as he grew from child to man.

Let's imagine a possible scenario for what might have happened, even if Luke offers no detail. We gain a clear understanding of our narrative when we examine the travel patterns of Jewish families during the time of Jesus. Taking precise safety measures and strict precautions, the people traveled in caravans. Some men traveled ahead of the pack, the women and children in the middle, and other men brought up the rear of the traveling processional. Thus, when Jesus traveled neither with Mary or Joseph, neither parent worried. Mary knew that Jesus would soon reach adulthood as a man. Maybe she thought he traveled with the men to claim his emerging manhood. Joseph figured Mary wanted to hang on to Jesus' childhood as long as possible, so she encouraged Jesus to travel with the women and children. Or perhaps his parents assumed he traveled somewhere among friends and relatives. This kind of childcare arrangement remains foreign to modern parents, but in Jesus' time, relatives and friends relieved parents of some of the anxiety of having to constantly watch over their own children.

It upsets present-day readers when Luke informs us that Jesus' parents took three days to find him. Before we reprimand Mary and Joseph for their neglect and what some might denote as apparent lack of good parenting skills, it helps us to once again review the travel patterns of the time. It took one day to their camp, where they realized Jesus was missing. The couple spent another day traveling back to Jerusalem. Mary and Joseph spent the third day searching for Jesus and eventually found him in the temple.

Reading the text, we detect supposed rudeness on the part of Jesus as he engaged his mother in conversation. Jesus said, "Why were you searching for me?" In his question, though, Jesus simply stated the obvious. His parents wasted their time searching in the homes of relatives and friends in Jerusalem as Jesus yearned to be in the house of God. Jesus pointed to his true destiny and his need to be present in the place where learned men possessed the skills to shape and nurture that destiny.

Luke paints for us a picture of Jesus at a crucial time in his life as he struggled with his conflicting loyalties between family and God. God won out. Jesus made it clears to his mother that he wanted to stay in Jerusalem rather than travel home. Surely his blunt honesty hurt Mary, just as the blunt honesty of our own children hurts us, but she recalled that she birthed an extraordinary child. At the end of the story, Luke softens the storyline. Jesus returned home, obeyed his parents, and grew in wisdom and strength.

Luke urges us to move ahead to embrace the voice of the child Jesus. His voice rang out in the temple, and the teachers' voices did not overshadow Jesus' voice. His voice demanded to be heard. His voice was strong, clear, and passionate. It produced question after question and answer after answer. Luke describes the voice as amazing. Yet at times, Jesus silenced his voice to listen, to hear, to comprehend, to absorb, and to process the teachings of wise men in his tradition. A golden moment for learning presented itself, and Jesus offered his full attention.

Jesus stood on the brink of manhood, ready to leave behind childhood. Still a child, however, he lifted his voice to dialogue with respected elders in his Jewish faith, men who taught and instructed him as well as listened to his voice. Jesus teaches modern readers and listeners of this story several valuable truths.

First, our children need wise teachers to instruct them in life, especially as they deal with religious and spiritual matters. Parents, grandparents, adopted grandparents Sunday school teachers, and friends constitute examples of these mentors and guides. Yet how can these individuals instruct children unless they themselves rigorously delve into God's Word and diligently study the scriptures? God calls us to become lifelong learners. *Just being caring adults does not qualify us to teach and instruct children.* Adults must constantly learn so children can turn to qualified, competent, educated biblical scholars, rather than inept learners.

Second, just as Jesus struggled with his own identity, children today struggle with their own identities, especially as they approach adolescence. The age of twelve in our society presents itself as a time of radical growth and change. The age surrounds children with rapid changes physically, emotionally, socially, and spiritually. Children emerge from childhood into the pressures of the teenage years. Caring adults offer these children support, time, encouragement, and direction. They understand that these young people struggle with their own sense of purpose and identity. They affirm these youth as beloved children of God, worthy in God and their eyes. These adults refrain from constant criticism, but lavish these children with praise and affirmation.

Yet these adults do not shirk from using necessary and sensitive discipline as needed. Guided discipline provides children with helpful boundaries and limits that lead to safety and security. When adults treat children with love and respect and enact loving discipline as needed, children grow into adolescents who view themselves as people of self-worth. The children live their lives filled with pride in their achievements, but are also aware of their limitations. They gradually claim and use their God-given gifts in ministry and service to others.

Third, Jesus models for us an important pattern in our learning. He invites us to use both our listening skills and our individual analysis. The teachers of the law prided themselves on their abilities to dialogue with their students about difficult theological concepts. Students sat in a circle at the feet of their rabbis to learn and discuss. Jesus sat, mesmerized by the stimulating teaching. Although a child filled with wisdom, he refused to monopolize the conversation. He respected his elders' knowledge, he recognized their authority, and he listened attentively. However, he possessed a great deal of insight himself, especially for a child. Jesus amazed the teachers with his sharp mind and intellectual and theological thinking well beyond his age.

Adults must create a learning environment for children today where they, like Jesus, feel welcome to express their opinions, without fear of ridicule. This happens when adults truly listen to children, value their opinion, affirm their ideas, and, if necessary, reshape their thinking into more positive channels. Children desire adult friends and mentors who offer them their own faith story and teach them biblical truths. These adults joyfully impart their knowledge to children. Caring adults not only offer helpful teaching, but model listening skills, so children learn how to become good listeners.

Parents should teach children to listen to those adults and mentors who can teach children biblical truths. In our Bible story, Jesus respected his Jewish leaders by listening to them. He knew that he could garner many ideas from their teachings. Parents must seek out positive role models for children, mentors who gladly share their biblical interpretation and help children learn about Bible stories. These mentors provide an atmosphere of welcoming and openness, an excellent environment in which children learn in positive and lasting ways.

Finally, Jesus reminds us of the importance of children's questions. Undoubtedly, Jesus asked many questions of the teachers of the Law. The children we know are full of questions, also. Children ask challenging questions, and we may feel inadequate and afraid to answer them. Always take the questions of children seriously. Do not ever laugh at them or deem them to be ridiculous. Children learn and grow spiritually by asking questions. When we take a child's question seriously, we adults demonstrate our respect for the child.

In the confirmation class at Connell Memorial United Methodist Church, Pastor Paul allowed his confirmation students to ask questions about religious matters. Through their conversations with their pastor and class members, students grew in their faith.

Often it helps adults to take time to ponder and study the question the child asks. That way, adults make sure they truly comprehend what the child is asking. Otherwise, an adult might end up giving an answer that the child really does not want to know or answering the question in ways that are not helpful to the child. Adults tend to give a much longer and more detailed answer to children's questions than is usually necessary. Being sure we understand the question helps us give an adequate and concise answer, rather than a long, detailed explanation that falls beyond a child's intellectual, emotional, and spiritual grasp. *Be careful to avoid giving a child more information that he or she is ready to process.*

Adults aid themselves in the skill of answering questions when they ask children what they think. Get their opinion before answering, because this often gives you a clue to what the child is really asking and what he or she wants to know. Probing the child guides adults and points them toward an adequate answer. It is extremely important never to give a child an answer which you are not sure is accurate. Be honest. Admit to the child what you do not know. Children understand that no one person holds all the answers to life's questions. Do not be afraid to tell children you do not know all of the answers, but then do your best to find help and information from other sources, and get back with the child on what you discover.

Jesus teaches us that children are spiritual beings. True wisdom and valuable knowledge involve a lifelong process of learning, answering questions, listening, and discerning. Childlike images of God are powerful and influence us throughout a lifetime. In Jesus' ever-expanding life experiences, including that of his time in the temple, he reshaped his image of God in light of what he learned from the authorities and his own life journey. The scriptures tell us that Jesus grew in knowledge, wisdom, and stature. He grew physically, mentally, emotionally, and spiritually. We rejoice when the Bible story informs us of this truth. We also rejoice when we too develop into whole people, children who please God with our wisdom.

QUESTIONS FOR REFLECTION AND DISCUSSION

1. Discuss some of the difficulties you have with the Bible story of Jesus being lost and then found by his parents in the temple. What elements of the story disturb you or challenge your faith?

2. How do you see both the humanity and divinity of Jesus depicted in the Bible story?

3. Who have been the great teachers in your life? Name them, and offer a prayer of thanksgiving for their influence.

4. What theological questions would you ask of great teachers?

5. How can you take seriously the questions of children?

6. How can congregations teach children to love and respect the church in the same way Jesus loved and respected the temple?

7. Names ways in which you see the children you know growing in wisdom and strength. Share ways you can help children grow physically, emotionally, and spiritually.

8. Name some wise teachers in your congregation, especially those who relate well to children. Offer a prayer of thanksgiving for these teachers.

9. How can churches create a learning environment where children can express their opinions, yet also learn to listen carefully to their teachers and mentors?

10. How would you share your faith story with a child? What story do you have to share, and how could you put the story into words that children would understand and appreciate?

Bibliography

"Cats Control Humans with High-pitched, Urgent-sounding Meows, Study Finds." *New York Daily News*, July 14, 2009. http://articles. nnydailynews.com/2009-07-14/entertainmnenbt/1792051_1_cat-s- purr-cry-or-meow-humans.

Couzens, Fred. "Boy Collects Blankets for Homeless at Rescue Mission," *Downtown View*. http://www.viewnews.com/2008/VIEW-Dec-09-/ Tue-2008/downtown/25523806.htmnl.

Espiritu, Joseph. "Laguna Niguel Boys Collect Blankets, Jackets for the Homeless." *OC Register.com*. http://articles.ocregister.com/2010-12- 20/news/25294129_1_blankets-jackets-collection-drive.

Fleming, Nic. "Hungry Cats Trick Owners with Baby Cry Mimicry." *New Scientist,* July 13, 2009. http://www.newscientist.com/article/ dn17455-hungry-cat-trick-owners-with-baby-cry-mimicry.html.

"Jeboash of Judah." http://en.wikipedia.org/wiki/Jehoash_of_Judah.

"Joash, King of Judah." http://www.little_folks.com/joash_king_of_ judah.htm.

"Josiah." http:en.wikipedia.org/wiki/Josiah.

"St. Joseph's Children's Hospital Announces Kids Are Heroes Winners." *St Joseph's Children's Hospital*, December 14, 2010. http://www.facebook. com/note.php?note_id=178332495528663.

"The Dalai Lama." http://www.the-dalai-lama.com/.

"Tutankhamun." http://en.wikipedia.org/wiki/Tutankhamun.

Endnotes

1. "Kids are Heroes," *St. Joseph's Children's Hospital,* http://www.sjbhealth.org/body_childrens.cfm?id=368.

2. "St.Joseph's Children's Hospital Announces Kids Are Heroes Winners," December 14, 2010, http://www.facebook.com/note.php?note_id=178332495528663.

3. Nic Fleming, "Hungry Cats Trick Owners with Baby Cry Mimicry," *New Scientist,* July 13, 2009.

4. "Cats Control Humans with High-pitched, Urgent-sounding Meows, Study Finds," *New York Daily News*, July 14, 2009.

5. Nic Fleming, "Hungry Cats Trick Owners with Baby Cry Mimicry," *New Scientist*, July 13, 2009.

6. "Tutankhamun," http://en.wikipedia.org/wiki/Tutankhamun.

7. Ibid.

8. "Jeboash of Judah," http://en.wikipedia.org/wiki/Jehoash_of_Judah.

9. "Joash, King of Judah," http://www.little_folks.com/joash_king_of_judah.htm

10. "Jeboash of Judah," http://en.wikipedia.org/wiki/Jehoash_of_Judah.

11. "The Dalai Lama," http://www.the-dalai-lama.com/

12. "Josiah," http://www.en.wikipedia.org/wiki/Josiah.

13. Ibid.

14. Ibid.

15. Ibid.

16. Fred Couzens, "Boy Collects Blankets for Homeless at Rescue Mission," *Downtown View*.

17. Joseph Espiritu, "Laguna Niguel Boys Collect Blankets, Jackets for the Homeless," *OC Register.com*.

All websites most recently accessed on October 15, 2011.